This book was commissioned in response to the exhibition *Living with Buildings* curated by Emily Sargent at Wellcome Collection. The exhibition explores the pivotal role of design and urban planning in human health and examines how the structures that surround us shape our mental and physical health, in both positive and negative ways.

wellcome collection

WELLCOME COLLECTION is a free museum and library that aims to challenge how we think and feel about health. Inspired by the medical objects and curiosities collected by Henry Wellcome, it connects science, medicine, life and art. Wellcome Collection exhibitions, events and books explore a diverse range of subjects, including consciousness, forensic medicine, emotions, sexology, identity and death.

Wellcome Collection is part of Wellcome, a global charitable foundation that exists to improve health for everyone by helping great ideas to thrive, funding over 14,000 researchers and projects in more than seventy countries.

wellcomecollection.org

LIVING WITH
BUILDINGS

Christ Church, Spitalfields. Leon Kossoff.

LIVING WITH BUILDINGS

And Walking with Ghosts

On Health and Architecture

IAIN SINCLAIR

[signature]

P
PROFILE BOOKS

wellcome
collection

First published in Great Britain in 2018 by
Profile Books Ltd
3 Holford Yard
Bevin Way
London
WC1X 9HD
www.profilebooks.com

Published in association with Wellcome Collection for the
exhibition *Living with Buildings* curated by Emily Sargent.

**wellcome
collection**

183 Euston Road
London NW1 2BE
www.wellcomecollection.org

1 3 5 7 9 10 8 6 4 2

Typeset in Sabon by MacGuru Ltd
Printed and bound in Great Britain by Clays Ltd, Elcograf S.p.A.

A CIP catalogue record for this book is
available from the British Library.

ISBN 978 1 78816 046 9
eISBN 978 1 78283 446 5

FSC
www.fsc.org
MIX
Paper from
responsible sources
FSC® C018072

For Steve and Joan Dilworth, makers of place.

And Rebecca Hind, her fire windows.

Contents

MOVE
Christ Church: The Sickness and the Shadow   3
Ex-Voto Detour   27

FURTHER
John Evelyn's Mulberry Tree   43
Golden Lane   62
Radiant City   84

OUT
Southampton Water   113
Pilgrims, Herders and Hermits   128
Spitalfields: *Scintilla*   149

Select Bibliography   169
Acknowledgements   173
List of Illustrations   175
Living with Buildings: an exhibition   179
Index   181

'Descartes said all our ills come from a man being unable to sit alone, quietly, in a room.'

James Sallis

'He could walk. He walked.'

Joseph Conrad

POLICE, BY THE COUPLE, one standing back, came to the door. The first pair, interrupting our Sunday lunch, wanted witnesses to a kidnapping that might or might not have happened outside the local school. The second, late in the evening when the chain was on, were careful to check the address, the number. Unusually, they had turned out to deal with a reported intrusion. Local elections were imminent.

Nothing came of these tentative investigations. Uniforms we hadn't seen in forty years were pursuing crimes reported in another life. They were as bemused by this as we were. The original burglars had retired to Loughton and were driving minicabs. The 'kidnappers' were sold out, beaten to the floor, cuffed and dragged away.

And that's how it is with buildings and health. It might be centuries before potential detectives identify the source of the infection. Rooms, houses, flats, estates: they provide an unreadable richness of layered histories. But the instinct, however posthumous, however disorientating, remains: to balance the equation and close the case. Listen. The wronged dead are already tapping at our windows.

MOVE

Christ Church: The Sickness and the Shadow

'But most of the patients' notes are marked "Not for resus!"'
David Widgery

MUCH OF THE RUBBISH coming through my letterbox these days, now that the estate agents have flatlined, pitches funeral insurance. 'When you've lived a long life, there is no avoiding the sad reality, we have to plan for our passing on.' After more than seventy fortunate years on earth, when gravity is applied, there is always a faint, unsourced smell of charring fat. Chill anticipation of something far worse, shadows detaching themselves from once familiar buildings, asserting their independence before fading away.

I had been advised by a trusted source to inspect a set of newly installed watercolour paintings by Rebecca Hind, a reredos triptych in Christ Church, Spitalfields. On my next free afternoon, I obeyed. That was in 2010. I always intended to return, to take a more measured look. Now, invited to consider the relationship between built environments and the health of those who lived in them, the particular catch of light in my memory of the Hind paintings became critical. I needed to get back, but there were detours, other voices, other duties. Years passed. I found myself plodding towards the church door only when those big iron gates were locked. Or television lighting rigs were being wheeled into place by crews who had started the day too early to know where they really were. Catering trucks were the only reliable geographic fact.

It is our melancholy fate, as higher animals, to carry our ills, while searching for somewhere to plant them. Better, I felt, to be outside, on the move, eyes cast down, swerving the shit, stooping painfully after useless coins, gleaning and gathering, but not gazing up at remote figures in high windows, or the mortal shiver in the crowns of London plane trees. We chew over old hurts and project a future that is already used up – while the significant other, the viral messenger, sleeping partner, parasite, alien-friend, waits to announce herself: a twinge here, a dry cough, cold hands, stiff back, toes that refuse to clench. Let the doctors keep their verdicts until we're gone.

There is liberation in shutting the door behind us and striking out. Released from the sleep chamber where subconscious warnings play and tease their dream cinema, another night survived, we are mad to pitch into weather and landscape, so that what is left of the tattered rags of our common humanity must be shared with sorry derelicts, embattled survivors in the holes and cracks of an indifferent city. Even the dying obey the instinct to crawl into some rude shelter. But they are only hiding from their own powerlessness. So we walk away, while we can, in the superstitious belief that the ugly thing will not find us out. Our unmediated journey, beginning with a first hesitant step, protects us from immediate termination of contract: not today, not now, not yet, not until this new pilgrimage, the final of final programmes, is done.

'CARCINOMA, METHADONE, DIABETES, depression, miscarriage and angina have poured down as unremittingly as the weather,' wrote David Widgery in his essay, 'The Doctor is Sick', published in *Esquire* in 1991. General practitioners back then, still subject to the quasi-naval discipline of hospitals with eight dining rooms where different grades of staff never had to mingle, and green rooms with more desperate clients than can be registered as they wave their numbered tickets, were anathematised by tabloid journalists and bullying media moguls for threatening to speak out, or to take industrial action, against slashed budgets, rationalised refuges and rising tides of managerial bullshit. Doctors, male and female, had more to worry about than their caste titles and official designations.

Widgery, a Hackney-based physician and radical, an early US traveller/recorder, Beat enthusiast, contrarian, tried to keep a written record – against impossible hours worked, against carbon-dioxide commutes down roads clogged with construction traffic for the emerging Canary Wharf towers – of his experiences in Gill Street, a medical practice tucked alongside Nicholas Hawksmoor's imposing Portland stone temple, Saint Anne's. The sharp-angled church was a white battleship whose periscope tower, before recent interventions, was visible to incoming vessels on the Thames: an established London marker.

The doctor is remembered by a plaque in the garden beyond the churchyard. 'As a socialist and writer his life and work were an inspiration in the fight against injustice.' Words cut on slate honour the man who 'practised locally'. That is the key: locality. Widgery was embedded. Seen on film, he *moves*; he bristles, he engages. It appears, in television documentaries of that time, that the doctor regarded the buildings themselves as the enemy: malpractice and politic short-termism incubating rogue pathologies, tapping the sweats and fevers of migrant generations. And favouring impoverished and disenfranchised clients with the sickness of the system. The doctor, who was also a poet, made it his task to snare disease as a metaphor for the failures of the social contract.

In a photograph taken when he braved the 'forgotten' St

Vincent's House on St Saviour's Estate, the doctor's right arm is gauzed and bandaged. Walking home from the bus stop, at the end of a long and weary day, he was assaulted by four black youths. He 'left a goodish sample of epidermis on the pavement of Richmond Road'. Widgery wasn't obliged to experience the glamourised grot of *London Fields* by Martin Amis. He'd just been mugged there. He was hauled through the gutter by the strap of his medical briefcase. The twilight assailants got away with a blue convenience-store bag, a bottle of cheap plonk and a dirty shirt.

On call, the doctor's modest car is raided like a delivery van. Bicycles are barely pushed up the garden path before they're gone. Car radios, until they are left as gaping wounds in the dashboard, scream for a smarter class of wreck, a brief appearance in the recycling bins of Kingsland Waste market.

Widgery is summoned to the smoke-thick den of an extended but unlanguaged family, new arrivals from Bangladesh or Vietnam, where a young child, not yet immune to the microclimate, responds with bouts of spectacular projectile vomiting. We are ghosts talking to ghosts. The city is undone. Housing is the infirmity. Innocent carriers, risking everything in transit, are blamed.

As early as 1974, the promise of future towers justified a death certificate for overwhelmed but still functioning East London hospitals. The prognosis was poor. The managers couldn't manage anything beyond their own dissolution. Established hospital-estates, like St Clement's in Mile End Road, were a cartography of unquiet memories, pain smears, tiled corridors saturated in muffled sounds; the whisper of phantom wheels, bad news delivered in a steady voice.

'Memory of a memory of a memory,' said Lee Harwood, who spent a few grim months as a patient in the secure hospital colony, divorcing his cells from heroin, and absorbing the bitter essence of his capture by place. Here was a precise but provisional terrain in which the poet opened himself to the pathology of the city: tender collisions were arranged in expectation of the heart fluttering, missing the next beat, or catching the latest mortality telegram delivered from between the sticky pages of a retired book in the local history library in Bancroft Road. If hospitals are constructed as industrial plants for containing, manufacturing and focusing the sickness, they are better avoided. Libraries are more subtle, fingerprints and saturated sweat are left for generations on unopened pages. Tubercular wraiths, let in from the street, huddle around austerity-era radiators coughing over friable newspapers. Obituaries are hot news. You are not dead until they tell you that you are dead. In hospitals and libraries everybody is learning how to wait. Time is sucked from sick rooms like precious oxygen. Sit too long and you will never move again.

Another damaged London wanderer, the name character of W. G. Sebald's *Austerlitz*, experiences, after a collapse in Alderney Street, 'three weeks of mental absence' in St Clement's hospital, where he has been inserted, like a returned volume, among the sheets of a narrow bed in one of the male wards. Austerlitz processes the endless corridors, 'desolate and weirdly contented' on the palliative drugs he has been fed, peering through dirty windows at the fecund wilderness of Tower Hamlets cemetery. He is trapped within a structure – part prison, part asylum, part barracks (the keepers are prisoners too) – built to facilitate confusion. Patients arrive at the hospital gates with their undiagnosed but interesting problems as the price of entry.

Keep walking, Sebald implies, one step in front of another, so that the diagnosis allocated to you, and confirmed by experts, will never break cover. Austerlitz knows nothing beyond 'the four burnt-out walls of his brain'. Abolished names and legends in the cemetery cohabit with ivy-choked angels. Stonemasons have chipped and laboured to reference marine tragedies, industrial accidents, named babes who never learned to crawl.

Dr Widgery, in the conflicted condition of writer and physician, was well placed to engage with the wet-brained alcoholics and street-performing vagrants who sometimes encroached on the Limehouse Health Centre. He was aware of the risks taken by doctors who chose to write, or writers who dabbled in medicine. He spoke of the poet William Carlos Williams, a general practitioner in Paterson, New Jersey, as an exemplar: a man who knew how to watch and wait. The doctor kept a prescription pad handy, on which to seize the moment. Williams scribbled his notes for subsequent scoring on the practice typewriter, before the day's work began: the never-ending consultations, the hesitant confessions to be unpicked, the expectant mothers. All that history to be absorbed and processed before his own stroke, insult to the brain, narrowed the horizons.

Alfred Döblin (*Berlin Alexanderplatz*), Brecht, Conan Doyle and Bulgakov were also cited. Widgery did not mention the perverse genius Louis-Ferdinand Céline, who was visited in paranoid retreat at Meudon, a south-west suburb of Paris, by Allen Ginsberg and William Burroughs. Burroughs, like J. G. Ballard, dabbled with medical studies, acquiring a forensic eye and a taste for formaldehyde in the morning. Surgeons, for Burroughs, were virtuosi, carving and drilling and joking, treating their victims like stooges dragged on stage by a malicious comedian. Céline, by the time the Beat poets arrived at his gate, had seen his madness, pricked by First War wounds, shrapnel in the head, seep into the bombed ruins around him; a flight to the east, Berlin and the Baltic, ending in prison and disgrace.

Barry Miles, in his biography of Ginsberg, says that Céline 'was dressed almost as a *clochard*, in three moth-eaten sweaters'. The shamed doctor was still in business but his diminishing list of patients now regarded him as a man condemned, a manifestation of the sickness of the years of German occupation. The language virus had undone him. 'There was brown mold under his fingernails.'

LONDON *CLOCHARDS* IN THE SNOW, with punched-pillow, medieval faces, warming broken-knuckled hands over pallet-board fires, feature on the cover of Markéta Luskačová's *Photographs of Spitalfields* (1991). A nocturnal gang of strategically aligned substance abusers. A tactical collective, mostly male and tribal, battling to survive in the vanishing hinterland between the City and the ghetto. Hardened men with deleted histories make it their business to self-medicate, to keep away from punitive charity and the buildings where the sickness lodges; where it has lodged since the verminous days of Jack London and *The People of the Abyss* (1903). The photographs in the early editions of London's book, many taken by the author himself, operate in a very different way to the crafted inserts in a book by W. G. Sebald. Sebald manipulates his text: it is easy to imagine him counting the words, designing a single sheet as an illuminated block. The Sebaldian image, sometimes copied and recopied, authenticates a teasing fiction. Found postcards dictate their own terms. Jack London's photographs are reportage. They confront the ambiguities of the prose and its status as confession or contrivance.

After being led into teeming, rancorous hovels, as tourist-reporter not medical practitioner, London discovers scenes that David Widgery later experienced. He recorded poverty caves loud with colours and characters seductive to writers: author as diagnostician. 'His skin an unhealthy colour, body gnarled and twisted out of all decency, contracted chest, shoulders bent prodigiously from long hours of toil, and head hanging heavily forward and out of place.' Prognosis as prophecy. Flesh as an avatar of poverty.

Whitechapel rookeries cough and retch. 'I could make out fish and meat bones, garbage, pestilential rags, old boots, broken earthenware, and all the general refuse of a sty.'

The sturdy Californian adventurer, head and shoulders above those who guide him, asks to be led back, not into an unexplored zone of the titular abyss but into a literary fable: 'the site of the slums where lived Arthur Morrison's *Child of the Jago*'. Purpose-built tenements, for those who could afford them, after the original underclass warrens, with all the consumptions of the dispossessed, had been demolished and their occupants dispersed. The new structures around Arnold Circus boasted a clean bill of health: incomers were issued with rent books and the obligation of scrubbing the stairs. Only the fit and deloused could take up residence in buildings designed to advertise the clean skins and superior sanitation of those who could afford to rise in the world.

WITH HIS CAMERA AND NOTEBOOK, Jack London circles Hawksmoor's Christ Church. He does not look up at the portico, the threatening mass of columns, ledges and alcoves. The Mayan dagger of the steeple. He does not step beyond the defensive railings. He stays outside. A photograph from distance, in which men are sprawled, sick or drunk, against the unforgiving hull of blackened stone, and women are upright, still in the game, perky in straw hats against the railings, has a helpful caption: 'In the Shadow of Christ's Church, I Saw.' That apostrophe is a curling finger of blame. A signalled sarcasm. Church without deity. The formidable conceit of this established structure, London suggests, reveals nothing more than an alembic in which to cook the physical ills of the district, to cull the unworthy, the unbelievers. The non-conformists. Christ Church excludes those who have most need of its grudging benevolence.

'Where the shadow falls, all that is mine,' Hawksmoor seems to say. London's lost ones – those of the city and of the American writer with the same (adopted) name – settle, men and women together, on a circlet of bench around a plane tree in the barren rug of park to the south of the church. The park is a waiting room for sanctioned

'In the Shadow of Christ's Church, I Saw.' Jack
London, *The People of the Abyss*.

'A chill raw wind was blowing, and three creatures huddled
there sleeping or trying to sleep.' Jack London.

outpatients, hawking, scratching, but staying in the honest, filthy London air, lungs shredded and cuttlefish black.

Inside Christ Church, down in the crypt, is an oozing mire of Spitalfields corpses, pressing on each other, mulched with rotten wood, foul cerements and linen rags: sad vanities as comforters for a theoretical afterlife. Failed charms against oblivion. London's outsiders know and fear closing doors, unwelcoming interiors: they stay outside.

'The shadow of Christ's Church falls across Spitalfields Garden,' Jack London wrote, 'and in the shadow of Christ's Church, at three o'clock in the afternoon, I saw a sight I never wish to see again … Grass only grows here, and it is surrounded by sharp-spiked iron fencing, as are all the parks of London Town, so that homeless men and women may not come in at night and sleep upon it.'

The American, this squalor tourist, enters Itchy Park like a house surgeon making his brisk ward rounds. 'On the benches on either side was arrayed a mass of miserable and distorted humanity … It was a welter of rags and filth, of all manner of loathsome skin diseases, open sores, bruises, grossness, indecency, leering monstrosities, and bestial faces.'

There was no healing sleep in the short, interrupted night. The morning shadow of Hawksmoor's stone steepletree was the call to movement, expulsion from the garden. The sick ones doze. They share their dreams, whatever moments of oblivion they can manage. *But it is always safer to be outside.* The crypt, in time, will be decanted and scoured, bodies arranged across the floor of the empty church – before the vaulting space can be heritaged, curated, tasked with generating an income stream. Before its malignancy can be exposed in conspiracy comics and blockbuster films. The London sickness, the rough sleepers intuit, is a privilege of architecture: it lodges in churches and hospitals and schools. It lodges in the palaces and mansions and railway suburbs from which they are excluded.

It is 'by the portico of Christ's Church, where the stone

'View in Spitalfields.' Jack London.

pillars rise towards the sky', and where 'whole rows' of men are trying and failing to sleep, that Jack London delivers his verdict. 'A lung of London ... nay, an abscess, a great putrescent sore.' The visitor to the lower depths can now burn his borrowed clothes. His photographs, faces blurring when the subject turns away, are grounded. They begin with people on the street; with tenements, charity shelters and churches as backdrop, evidence for a polemic.

In the accepted 'view' of Spitalfields – a corner of the market as seen from the portico of Christ Church – the seething mass of humanity is frozen: lamp-post lounger, pavement squatter, carter, predestined strider, hands-in-pockets philosopher. And all of them quite oblivious to the General Gordon Temperance Hotel. And to the new building that will replace it. And to the building that will replace the replacement. And to the compulsive façadism of the twenty-first century, where boasted legacy is a curtain of quotations, behind which yet more empty apartments can be assembled for the online property catalogue. And fines paid to cover a shortfall in affordable housing.

Jack London's gloss is ugly and eugenicist: 'A breed strikingly differentiated from their masters' breed, a pavement folk, as it were, lacking strength and stamina. The men become caricatures of what physical men ought to be, and their women and children are pale and anaemic, with eyes ringed darkly, who stoop and slouch, and are twisted out of all shapeliness and beauty.'

'Deteriorated stock,' he concludes, 'left to undergo further deterioration.'

The ultimate metaphor in *The People of the Abyss* is mulched from the chimney and the ullage cellars of Truman, Hanbury and Buxton, the Quaker brewers, the vanished philanthropists of Brick Lane. 'Those that remain are the lees, and they are segregated and steeped in themselves ... They have dens and lairs into which to crawl for sleeping purposes, and that is all.'

OUR GREAT CONTEMPORARY PAINTER of this territory, Leon Kossoff, came at Christ Church from another angle entirely. He grew up near Arnold Circus among the reefs of tidy public housing that replaced the Old Nichol rookeries. He stood at the mouth of Fournier Street, and then crouched, to resurrect a child's awed but responsive strike at the rearing columns. He dignifies the structure as an unstable organic form. A buttery, slithering mass of many mysterious apertures but no point of entry. Kossoff does not stray into the fenced garden. He makes his preliminary drawings – stupendous dashes, diagnostic marks, whipping lines of charcoal and chalk, the firm vertical strokes of the Tuscan columns challenged by zigzag hatchings – from the north side, as he comes down, once more, from his childhood home. These drawings are heroic captures from the tumble of a frail craft about to be dashed against stupendous rocks, or swept headlong into the wash of Fournier Street. The hieratic building, a fanciful history of architecture in one stack, period lofted on period, sways at anchor. And sheers away from the witness. The tip of a stone mast before the raft of vision is overwhelmed.

Paul Moorhouse in his Tate Gallery publication, *Leon Kossoff* (1996), says that the painter's enthusiasm for the motif, after previous struggles, was rekindled by a reading of *Hawksmoor*, the Peter Ackroyd novel published in 1985. Kossoff has spoken of how Arnold Circus looked and felt, on one August day of dusty sunlight. It was 'like the London of Blake's Jerusalem'. The abnegation to place and the plurality of time manifests as a psychic seizure: 'The urgency that drives me to work is not only to do with the pressures of the accumulation of memories and the unique quality of the subject on this particular day but also with the awareness that time is short.' And not just, as the painter implies, for a London threatened by the presumption of City towers, but for his own health and strength. The area's continued resistance is encoded in the thrust of Christ Church's spectacular elevation. 'It is by its monumental flight into unimpeded space that we remember this building.'

WALKING ONE AFTERNOON from Bishopsgate towards Toynbee Studios on Commercial Street, and emerging from Artillery Lane into White's Row, I was astonished to discover that the multi-storey car park covering the site of the 'final' Ripper murder had disappeared, along with the rest of the buildings on the south side of Spitalfields Market. And as a result, when the dust settled, there was a new prospect of Christ Church. The demolition would have been approved by Hawksmoor. Now at last his church could be seen as a freestanding sculpture, undiminished by commerce and human traffic. I don't remember seeing a drawing or photograph that presented the building from this side – without much of the south façade being hidden by the trees of Itchy Park. The tanned steel engraving from a drawing by B. Cole that hung above my desk isolated Christ Church from its surroundings, presenting it, in afternoon shadow, as on a beach of smoothed cobbles, left by a retreating sea.

The sky had thickened and rusted in an eclipse caused by sandstorms in the Sahara. But the prospect was entirely orthodox, made from Kossoff's favoured position. The body of the church is dramatically foreshortened to throw emphasis on the priapic tower and steeple.

Excited by the new vision delivered by developers, but appreciating that it would soon be lost, I wrote to Kossoff. He replied, thanking me, and saying: 'I haven't been able to get around much lately so I haven't seen what's happening at Christ Church but this week-end my son will drive me there – I am prepared for a shock.'

The Hackney medical man David Widgery, whose combative energies derived in some part from the determination to make up for years lost to childhood polio, recognised and celebrated the hustling, eccentric (and doomed) market life captured in Markéta Luskačová's Spitalfields photographs. The doctor is not a eugenicist like Jack London. He hymns Hawksmoor's church as 'marvellously intimidating', but he identifies a dissenting strain in the lineage. Like Kossoff, Widgery calls up William Blake as his witness: Londoner and artisan, street prophet in the red cap of liberty.

'Going, going, gone ... the corporate monoliths of business architecture, ugly by day, deserted at night, will continue their relentless obliteration of the ancient street patterns of the East End as the City lays claim to what it once cast out,' Widgery says. Buildings without souls, empty and 'under offer', announce 'the return of the scourges of malnutrition, tuberculosis, alcoholism and psychotic illness'.

As a physician-author, Widgery makes his rounds of streets recorded by the Czech photographer, 'noting the distinctive gait of the depot-medicated schizophrenic, the mannerist grimaces of the manic-depressive, the shuddering cough and luminous facies of pulmonary tuberculosis.'

Pre-fictional ghosts go about their business in a zone

of diminishing permissions, until they are noticed by artists, poets and photographers. Luskačová, a pioneer, engages with busking musicians, chicken butchers, unlicensed animal traders, fire-hugging *clochards* – and a man of the crowd, hands in pockets, with thick, helmet-tipped penis-nose (ahead of the Chapman Brothers), in Beckettian conversation with an umbrella-shrouded woman tethered to a spindly dog in a knotted sweater.

'It was as though Dave was aware he had limited time,' said Widgery's wife, Juliet Ash, introducing a posthumous collection, *Against Miserabilism* (2017). Christ Church, in its pomp, decline, resurrection, has siphoned time out of the equation, stolen it from the surrounding streets: for every generation there are new ancestors to be identified.

BEHIND THE LONDON STORIES we tell ourselves, in order to smother terrors that would otherwise nail our feet to the ground, is an agreement to let every walk dictate its own momentum towards the place it has to go. For me, striking south from Hackney, that place was often Christ Church. The other London churches by Hawksmoor, built between 1712 and 1731, are dedicated to saints: three male (George's-in-the-East, Alfege, George's Bloomsbury) and two female (Anne's Limehouse, Mary Woolnoth). But Christ Church, the third and last of the East London triumvirate, is the most complex and ambitious. It is established at a border point, facing the encroaching but never satisfied City and holding back the agitated thrust of the ghetto to the east. In balance, a sculptural masterwork, Christ Church achieves the illusion of being open and accessible to all, but also forbidding, proud beyond its moment, threatening to those who refuse to acknowledge its potency or who seek to exploit that current for their own trivial ends. Borrowing its title from the Oxford college attended by a number of the commissioners for the establishment of Fifty New Churches, Christ Church was always an interloper, a fortress against the spread of non-conformity among the labouring classes. It was built to *press*, to contain the deserving dead who could not be planted in local earth.

Or that is how some of the more astute clergymen saw it. They were renting subterranean ledges to respectable and solvent parishioners who would, for a price worth paying, be secured against the depredations of resurrectionists. Those humble body-snatchers were part of the local food chain, recycling useless cadavers as specimens for medical research, demonstration models for the teaching hospitals. They carted their scavenged product across town, the dirt brushed off and rags removed by their wives for resale. They touted still warm grave goods, receiving room to receiving room, negotiating with claret-beaked gatekeepers, while giving what small support they could, along their unsteady way, to publicans and chartered houses set up for the comfort and relief of travellers and workmen.

I carried these picaresque notions with me when I became a municipal garden-labourer, trimming the grass of two Hawksmoor churches, picking up shards of broken British sherry bottles, before retreating to Tower Hamlets Cemetery to write up my notes, in the summer of 1974. The city was sickening, but I was outside, working in the open air with a gang of others, proper gardeners who were in for the duration – with their gripes and wartime reminiscences and slow-burning, needle-thin roll-ups. Like David Widgery, in the Gill Street medical practice, I combined long hours navigating the riverside reaches, tidying up the mess and trying to find a quiet corner in which to transcribe my immediate impressions. Sketching against oblivion.

My journey to Limehouse was initiated on 4 February 1974 by the dream of a swollen, steel-dish moon crashing down on the city, burying itself in the tower of St Anne's. Here was a somatic tarot card predicting 'hidden enemies, danger, calumny, darkness, terror, deception, occult forces, error'. But it was much worse than that. The church became the lodestone of my health and sanity. Commercial Road speeded up like the aeon-devouring conclusion to William Hope Hodgson's *The House on the Borderland*. 'I feel ever the burning of this dread growth. It has covered all my right arm and side, and is beginning to creep up my neck. Tomorrow, it will eat into my face. I shall become a terrible mass of living corruption.'

According to my unstable and unresolved thesis, being outside and in motion was the surest way of postponing ill health – which might just as well be described as an imbalance of humours. My diagnosis was medieval. Which was not a bad place to start in this landscape. I was a prematurely failed medical student, my school science results were so hopeless that I never made it to the starting gate, but I came from two generations of practitioners. I grew up with consulting room chatter as background noise. I listened to my father who appeared to take his credo from Simenon's Maigret: 'Understand and judge not.' Let nature take its course with minimal intervention, especially the offer of packaged drugs from pharmaceutical salesmen handing out free pens and beakers with slogans. Never step *inside* a surgery – sick building, worse light – except in an emergency, bones sticking through flesh. Surgeries and waiting rooms have absorbed too many ills: the sniffling, sweating, bleeding and trembling. The fear. Avoid hospitals like the plague (they brew it with their unnatural temperatures). And make it back at the end of your walk to the desk, the room, the house where it is permitted to sit still. To wait, without fretting, for the words to find you out.

A few months into my gardening sabbatical and the original sickness theory was in tatters. Journals of the time record hay fevers, streaming eyes, the revenge of cut grasses. Half the sections I prepared – after escaping to a Dorset cottage in chill winter – for my 'Hawksmoor' book, *Lud Heat*, were about bodily collapse. I saw the attacks as a form of 'priestly prohibition'. I quoted the filmmaker/poet Stan Brakhage. 'He must cave-live, at least as one does in the concrete city, run from the hunt of the summer equinox, avoid all flowerings, sex, laughter, or other human excitements, and rest preferably in a squatting or other wakeful position cautious to eliminate his dreams.'

London was an excavated neolithic dream. St Anne's, doors locked, alcoves squatted by vagrant drinking schools, was a nightmare vision of the coming millennium. When an attempt was made by a sound recordist, hoping to compose a poetry programme for BBC Radio 3, the still unimproved crypt delivered a thick and dusty silence, underwritten by slow, choking breaths – as if the boat of the Limehouse church was sinking under Thames mud. 'Local pains block the ease of conduct in the world. What you suffer is the place you choose to live,' I wrote. 'When we understand the condition it no longer exists.'

This febrile concentration on the Hawksmoor churches, their alignments, the patterns they made across the economically submerged hamlets of East London, became a literal fever, English sunstroke: a malarial collapse dignified by visions derived from Robert Louis Stevenson, pursuit by relentless and unforgiving doubles.

'Dreams suffused by a peculiar shade of brown, something like that of sealskin.' Was the sickness located in the building itself, in its brooding, pre-Dockland limbo, or in our refusal to properly engage, to climb the steps, doff the cap, come inside? Join the absent congregation of voices.

CAROL WILLIAMS, a former Londoner now living in Sag Harbor, Long Island, read my Hawksmoor improvisations with alarm. Having considered the matter, she offered her solution to the perceived malignancy of Christ Church. She recalled Rudolph Steiner writing that 'in pre-Atlantean times memory was geographic … People who wanted to remember something had to go back to the place where it happened. The landscape was punctuated with little marker sticks to help them locate their memories.'

I felt that my compulsive fugue-drifts towards Christ Church were attempts to recapture a memory I could never bring into focus, perhaps the memory of something that had not yet happened. The church was not only the expression of faith in an architecture inclusive of earlier orders and apparently conflicted theologies, the relish for a more 'primitive' and purer form of Christianity, but an immaculately honed instrument for isolating some unidentified spirit. Be it social, economic, occult or viral, any attempt at prognosis was a stab in the dark.

Carol's father, Bronek Katz, an emigrant modernist from Poland, who trained as an architect with Walter Gropius, designed the Homes and Gardens Pavilion for the Festival of Britain at the South Bank in 1951. He also worked on aspects of the Bata shoe factory (and colonial estate) at East Tilbury, a site that never fails to intrigue those who come across it unexpectedly, while tramping between river and railway. Or searching for Joseph Conrad's farmhouse in Stanford-le-Hope. Bronek Katz as Mr Kurtz.

This career – Carol's father died after a heart attack while skiing in 1960 – was all too brief. Bauhaus programmes of light and space, in dialogue with British pragmatism, illuminated that brief post-war, Welfare State moment when the ideal of improved health by better design, better materials, more sunshine, more space in which to exercise, seemed achievable. Green oases among grey miles of rubble and ash and traumatised brick.

Katz translated his beliefs into domestic architecture. He realised a family home in Chepstow Place, Notting Hill. In the collection, *London, City of Disappearances* (2006), Carol wrote about the construction of the house and its subsequent history. 'LCC Rules (with which my left-wing father enthusiastically concurred) ordered a certain number of council houses to be built before the development of private property.' The Katz residence, Carol tells us, was 'the first private house (more guilt for him) built, after the war, in the then Borough of Kensington.' In every possible way, 'the house resisted darkness'.

And yet good health somehow evaded the benevolent paradigm: Bronek Katz died in Austria. His widow and the children moved to another property they had acquired for investment: 16 Chepstow Place. A house with a certain literary pedigree. It was the address of the 'depraved' Mr Malthus, a member of the Suicide Club in the story of that name by Robert Louis Stevenson. This was also the last secure refuge for the beached author and fading bohemian dandy Julian Maclaren-Ross, now sick and in retreat from the constant chase after cheques. He hid from his wife and creditors behind green-tinted spectacles. The consummate literary professional was too far gone for sustained work and no longer capable of being cranked up by the 'green bombs' to which he had become addicted: the old Beat Generation Times Square recipe from the forties – Benzedrine-soaked strips infused in weak coffee, broken from inhalers intended for asthma sufferers and hay fever victims. Unearned energy with a future bill to pay.

There was a neat twist in the plot that brought Maclaren-Ross to Chepstow Place, a gimmick he might have worked into one of his stories. In an earlier white-knuckle phase – and most were, between windfalls and fitful notoriety – he pitched a film to Alexander Korda and picked up £25. The project was titled *The Beast in View* – a quote taken, as Paul Willetts, the Maclaren-Ross biographer points out, from John Dryden. The proposed treatment was an adaptation of Stevenson's *The Suicide Club*. The conceit of the 1878 novella is that members of the club agree to kill each other. *The Beast in View* was never made. But Maclaren-Ross, when he squatted in the outer suburbs, on the sofa of Anthony Cronin, author of *Dead as Doornails*, took to making threatening phone calls as 'Mr Hyde'.

The route that led him to the flat in Chepstow Place, where the culmination of the long sickness of life was waiting patiently, was a liaison with Eleanor Brill, who worked for the Reuters news agency. Willets has a photograph of her, fur-trimmed coat, walking stick at the ready, distinctive eyebrows arched, promenading alongside, but keeping a safe distance from, another ruined dandy of the period, the poet and bibulous man of letters John Gawsworth, who has something of the affronted pout of Salvador Dalí after his moustache has been stolen in the night. They are heading for the pub, perhaps the Alma, close to Chepstow Place, where they were fit to drown by the glass with Maclaren-Ross and Charles Wrey Gardiner.

The tide turned. There was a modest repeat fee from the BBC. Along with a sudden tightening in the chest. Maclaren-Ross self-medicated on a bottle of decent brandy. Eleanor got him to hospital in Ladbroke Grove. But the old heart was done. His last words are reported as 'Graham Greene' and 'I love you'. Not in the same sentence. With a pause between.

KEEPING AWAY FROM HAWKSMOOR CHURCHES and illicit hay fever remedies dissolved in coffee cups, I was fit to take on work offered by Carol Williams as a painter/decorator in the Chepstow Place flat. Rude health and a willingness to come across to West London were my only qualifications for the job. I scratched at resistant paint and plaster for hours, inhaling the dust without absorbing any of the panache of Maclaren-Ross or the darker residues of Stevenson's *The Suicide Club*. Every morning, on my return, mug of coffee in hand, I contemplated the previous day's progress. And there was none. The original paintwork had returned in the night, refreshed, reborn, holding firm to a narrative of the room I would never be allowed to infiltrate or refine.

Snowflakes melted on the windows. At 1 p.m., precisely, the tapping started. Like a tell-tale heart. Like the heart of

Maclaren-Ross protesting against years of abuse, full-English breakfasts with amphetamine chasers, pimp cigars and sewers of Fitzrovian booze fuelling the pub performances necessary for securing the next tentative commission. The deathwatch tapping was not in the wall, but in the window, minor vibrations causing the snowflakes to weep and slither.

Down below, the guardians of the ground-floor flat, Donald and Pauline McWhinnie, in long coats, woollen caps and thick gloves, were playing their thirty minutes of constitutional table tennis. In total silence. With never a superfluous nod or gesture. McWhinnie was a friend and correspondent of Samuel Beckett. He directed Beckett's radio plays. The table tennis was performed to Beckett's austere and precise rules of engagement. I heard echoes of J. G. Devlin as 'Mr Rooney' in the version of *All that Fall* that McWhinnie produced for the Third Programme in 1957. 'On the other hand, I said, there are the horrors of home life, the dusting, sweeping, airing, scrubbing, waxing … Nothing, I said, not even fully certified death, can ever take the place of that.'

Heading at dusk for the tube, I scanned boards advertising the latest murder, a conventionally gay man with royal connections stabbed, or beaten, or choking to death on his own blood. The details, with tabloid variants, were vague, hinting at inevitable punishment for the crime of being a writer. And for inviting a young man of the wrong class, like a cocky rogue out of Joe Orton, in from the cold. The only firm fact was the address. The murder chamber was in Ladbroke Grove, a short step from Chepstow Place.

James Pope-Hennessy, who once shared a flat with Guy Burgess, was rumoured to have received a large US advance for a biography of Noël Coward. Three Piccadilly rent boys with whom the author had previous dealings roughed up their patron and inserted a hairnet, forcibly, into his throat. There were no caches of spare loot to be found. Literary advances arrive, well skimmed, in small tranches, not black bags. The typescript, spattered with blood (according to conspiracy theorists), on which Pope-Hennessy was working was yet another biography, published posthumously and unrevised, of Robert Louis Stevenson.

When, in due course, Carol read my wild theories based around the force field of the Hawksmoor churches, and the occult conjurings seemingly authored by Christ Church in *White Chappell, Scarlet Tracings*, she had a solution: bury the whole structure in earth, let it grass over. Make a new mound to replace the defensive hill, heaped up at the time of the English Civil War, beside the Royal London Hospital in Whitechapel. A mysterious earthwork of spiral pathways with a chambered core. An elevation from which to appreciate the emerging city and the busy river.

But I had my own defensive magic in place, the routine of walking unresolved problems out into the city, eavesdropping on random incidents, forcing connections, and carrying annotations and photographs back to the house in which I had lived for fifty years. If we are to sustain a relationship with the buildings that precede us, we must solicit their tolerance of our intrusion. Structures ripped down leave a cloud of active dust. New builds are hungry for narrative. When that equation falters, we sicken, and search for scapegoats among the developers and architects. But the buildings and their interior spaces, bedrooms, corridors, kitchens, become evolving self-portraits, visions of how we see our better selves. Working or resting, we shape who we are, and are shaped, in exchange, by the walls that contain us. Some of the older tribes on this earth, indigenous peoples able to convert time into space, flow with the seasons, with their seminal rivers. Shelters are made and abandoned. Ancestors are always in attendance.

'Sicknesses, dreams, and ecstasies in themselves constitute an initiation,' Mircea Eliade said, 'that is, they transform the profane individual into a technician of the sacred.'

A London crow parked for a moment, just outside the window, on my neighbour's mossy slates, sated and belching on road-kill and fast-food droppings, gave me an old-fashioned stare, before taking off in disgust. Shamanism, he implied, is not for amateurs.

Ex-Voto Detour

'I have been out. I saw hospitals.'

Rainer Maria Rilke

MOVING NOW, WE ARE AFFECTED by the presence of individual buildings as by the trees of the forest. Each fossilised trunk its own history, each trunk part of a more complex organism: the city. Our traces are felt in the communication between buildings as they register our passage. The system is in precarious balance. Our moods adjust to reflections and shadows and the crowds that surge and flower, parading their neuroses. When my wife, recuperating, no longer accompanied me on a morning walk through a certain quiet street near Victoria Park, total strangers emerged from behind their windows and drawn curtains to ask what had happened. Was she well? Sleeping houses feed on the sugars of passerines, unconscious messengers.

IN SMEARED TWILIGHT, a dip of the shoulder south of Euston Road, clamping my lips to avoid the sour drench of stalled, snarling, emphysemic vehicles and the eternity of improvements bringing restless London to a shuddering halt in the underpass with its slow roll of overhead ad-porn, before the reef of hotels and terminal stations – and remembering John Evelyn's *Fumifugium*, his 1661 denunciation of noxious stinks trapped in the funnel of the Thames Valley – I rediscovered the magic of movement.

Above resistant pavements, I floated. That miraculously accessed network of walkable streets, close passages, curves, crescents, and permitted alleyways that are still there, outside time, offering, for whoever wants to experience it, narratives of a submerged and continuing city.

By now I should be dead. Or, by any reasonable accounting, coughing up my lungs in an isolation ward on the Dartford Marshes, a day's sail in a fever boat from the Isle of Dogs. But well-intentioned hospital colonies like Joyce Green on the Dartford Marshes, between sewage works and cemetery, supplied by regular infusions of workers who couldn't work (and their children), were no longer there. Blots on the OS map, ghosts of progress. The generous airing courts and suntraps were now shelters for rodents. I could only surmise, after so many years tramping the major traffic ditches and motorway fringes, that somehow, by regular homeopathic doses, my country-born immune system had learned to thrive on pollution. The pores might be clogged and scurf grey, the pouches of the lungs black and tarry, but they seemed to function. Just so long as they remained untested and unrecorded in the medical system. And so long as I kept well away from germ-free, open-plan offices, those temperature-controlled corporate conservatories wallowing in the wrong sort of light. Those suffering interior jungles with their immodest art-substitutes: both unfinished and overfinished. The hard Scandinavian chairs in nursery colours: canned salmon, loud yellow, grape and lime.

Hospitals, universities, *collections*: they are all about waiting. Securing a round table. Accessing the right screen. Postponed meetings to confirm the next meeting. These buildings are quotations that should never have been released from the catalogue. They are enclosed streets, the CGI version of Walter Benjamin's Parisian arcades: airless atria in which to put on time. There is a bell jar microclimate of lassitude and anxiety. World news is framed on a high screen (mute) like a devotional painting from the future. Being here, an accredited temporary migrant, you are insulated against harm. The suspended monitor is a superstitious offering to keep us safe from what is happening outside. The fires, the rubble. Post-traumatic child eyes. Undressed wounds. Feasting flies. The bombed hospitals accused of sheltering bombers.

Coming off the street, you will always encounter a melancholy security guard, shamed by ill-fitting uniform, paid to stand and yawn, before allowing the right sort of petitioner access to a reception island efficiently womanned by dispensers of laminated badges – who reluctantly concede an advance on blast-repelling barriers, card-activated non-revolving doors (supervised by more uniformed security). And all of it a humourless joke witnessed by surveillance cameras charged with providing content for unwatched screens. Unwatched unless the terrible thing happens. Again.

There was a meeting to attend in one of the smartest hangars on Euston Road. There are always meetings in flexible spaces serviced by refreshment stations where discounted coffee is released on contact with a contactless card. Today I was beginning to consider the Pepys Estate in Deptford. It was strange to be researching a downriver episode of social housing from the 1960s in a location that seemed to deny that such things had ever happened, except as case files. I thought of the helicopter jeremiads of John Betjeman from a poetically voiced documentary of that era. Oh dear! Oh dear! Those broken lifts! The pinched lives on the twentieth floor of a riverside block, a *slab*, unredeemed by prospects of nautical Greenwich and the distant hills. 'Caged halfway up the sky,' the poet moaned. He was talking about the latest high-rise towers, not the helicopter. Which, very wisely, he refused to enter. Deptford horrors were endured in an editing suite.

And then there were the social-realist captures of Tony

Ray-Jones, who seemed to be anticipating Ken Loach and Mike Leigh – the life of others – when he was commissioned to make a photographic record of the Pepys Estate: old men wearing their caps and trilbies on gravity-depressed sofas in low-ceilinged cabins, and estate kiddies at unsupervised riot on windswept concrete decks. The word *estate*, tried out in Deptford, came with its own heritage, summoning unreliable memories of cultivated gardens and private parks with grand-tour Roman statuary.

John Evelyn, the diarist and neighbourhood magnate of the Restoration period, enjoyed good health and kept clear of the surgeons who gave his friend Samuel Pepys such a rough ride in extracting a kidney stone the size of a tennis ball. Pepys was a hypochondriac with much to be hypochondriac about. When the mortal shadows came for Evelyn in 1682, the diarist made an inventory of Sayes Court and put his papers in order, while he waited stoically for the worst. He countered a series of unexplained fits, arriving upstream like dreadful intelligence from the City, by sitting inside a 'deep Churn or Vessell' and swallowing an infusion of thistle. The Restoration period, with its coffee-house conversations and newly founded Royal Society, was fertile ground for enlightened quackery and amateur experiments in disciplines still to be defined and regulated.

Seasonal plagues were purged in fire. And rational geometries proposed for a new city. Immigrants, economic or in flight from religious persecution, brought new ideas, new technologies. Both Evelyn and Pepys were elected as fellows of the Royal Society. They attended meetings and lectures. And demonstrations ranging from the art of veneering to the virtuoso dissection of opium-fed dogs. Sir Kenelm Digby, a naval commander and diplomat, floated the notion that wounds could be closed by first healing the weapon, stroking a 'sympathetic powder' along the edge of the blade that made the cut. Evelyn's language – he wrote much and aborted more – was as prolix and neurotically

Children playing on a raised walkway, Pepys Estate, Deptford.
Tony Ray-Jones, 1966.

Schoolboy in his living room posing for the photographer,
Pepys Estate, Deptford. Tony Ray-Jones, 1966.

discursive as my own struggle to lay out a coherent general theory about buildings and health.

BUT I COULDN'T SLINK BACK to my Hackney den without visiting other parts of this Euston Road building. If the unyielding exteriors of London solicit movement, interior spaces are about contemplation and self-reflection. About confrontation, business, the pitch. And waiting, drowning in stretched time. It's the difference between a speech and a silent prayer. A distinction eroded by the loud public discourse of fist-phone monologues; acceptably deranged pedestrians swearing, pleading, raging, loving. And praying.

I stepped outside and in through more revolving doors to the dedicated chamber where an eccentric collection of medical instruments, tribal artefacts and fetishes, mummies, ethnographic photographs and ex-voto paintings, was on free display. DISRUPT OUR SYSTEM ordered the big sign in the window. I would do my best to obey.

It was a disorientating experience to be outside, looking in on the open-plan conservatory, and seeing those coloured chairs, the discussions at round tables, and all of it happening in slow motion: an aspirational lifestyle for mere pedestrians to envy. *I could see myself,* still talking, gesturing, making no sense. I could see the two doctors, my father and his father (who died when I was a baby), as trapped spectres in the glass, posthumously summoned from some interminable debate, at BMA House in Tavistock Square, on the collapse of the National Health Service.

The way my immediate ancestors, up from Wales, navigated London was to lurch between duty and pleasure: museums, theatre, restaurants and department stores. They were eager to be informed, but weary of the weight of everything that was out there. Of London's mass, its mighty accumulations. Which was the way I felt as I circled the challenge of the Wellcome Collection trophies.

William Price of Llantrisant (1800–1893) MRCS, LSA, medical practitioner, in druidic costume, with goats. Price's cremation of the body of his son Iesu Grist in 1884 established the legality of cremation as a means of disposal of the dead in England and Wales.

I began with the paintings. Here was that bearded druid-surgeon, William Price of Llantrisant, about to cremate his son, Iesu Grist. On playing fields above a village in the Vale of Glamorgan. Attended by goats. Here were numerous episodes of surgery as performance. As ritual. Nuns. Martyrs. Cadavers. Orgies of the damned to excite the righteous. The blind leading the blind. There were primitive but touching receipts for the fortunate who had been granted dispensation from death or disease by making wild promises to a representation of the Virgin Mary.

To take the tour of this room is to expose oneself to a maelstrom of energies. One image feeds into the next. The cumulative potency of objects affected my breathing. There was, if you gave way to it, an obligation to experience all the pathologies on display. Like an owl fed on firelighters, I was burning up from the inside out. Disorientated, with heart racing, I rushed for the street.

SENSIBILITIES SHARPENED by the afterglow of argument, the way any successful exhibition must work, I became aware that there was a health benefit in walking through an area of London mined with hospitals, clinics, churches and colleges. This was, I suppose, a twenty-first-century reprise of Kenelm Digby, and a wink of appreciation for the Norwich physician and speculative essayist Sir Thomas Browne. Can we stay well, our humours in balance, by drifting around the miraculous potentialities built into the architecture of healing? Can the *presence* of a great hospital, the knowledge that it is there and in service, support the charge of unearned convalescence?

Sebald writes about Browne's fanciful metaphor of clammy white mist rising over the eastern counties of England from bodies freshly opened after death. The German author, trapped in a hospital bed, feels his own consciousness dissolving into the same milk, muffling the chatter of nurses, as he tries to untangle one of Browne's

From the Walworth Clinic (1937), prefiguring the National Health
Service, a translation of Cicero's *Salus populi suprema est lex*.

more labyrinthine paragraphs. Something of that sort lifted
my spirits too, as it always does, when I negotiate an untried
route through streets at the edge of my knowledge.

Striking out at random, I enjoyed the benefit of intimate
medical consultations I had never actually experienced,
in high rooms where timid footfall leaves no trace on the
carpet. Terrible verdicts are delivered in expensively modu-
lated voices from inner sanctums where consultees stare at
the landscapes in Dutch paintings, to be somewhere else,
and to stay there. Feel gratitude for the privilege of release
as you walk the night looking at the masked windows and
polished black cars waiting at the kerb with their dark spec-
tacled chauffeurs.

The entitlement of this area, a cordon sanitaire of re-
assurance for those who are wealthy and powerful enough
to suppress or deflect news of their mortality, led me to
consider the caste system of hospital visiting. Royalty, in
suites reserved for officers, receive no visitors: that would
be interpreted as a sign of weakness. The Firm carries on.
The Duke of Edinburgh is removed from public gaze, but
the Family are too busy to sit beside his bed. Sickness is
a condition of the poor, the disadvantaged. The confused
middle classes come to the shared ward for an hour, hiding

behind unsuitable fruit and awkwardness, wristwatches
exposed for a surreptitious glance. The people of the city,
immigrants and workers, move in around the stolen patient
en masse, bringing foil trays of food, gossip, rows. They
would get into bed with the sufferer if they could. They
do not trust the building or its servants. They remember
places where no provisions were supplied. The hospital
must be kept in life by their importation of the vitality of
the street.

Blind instinct ushered me through generously proportioned Georgian squares, town houses gleaming in coats
of freshly applied arsenic stucco, intimidating mansions
with blue-plaque beauty spots. (No satellite dishes here,
the plague buboes of poverty.) The heritage tributes are like
superglued Wedgwood dinner plates for departed benefac-
tors, superior physicians and statesmen, actors, musicians
and Bloomsburries. The secure gardens behind locked
iron fences are for key holders who have paid the tithe of
access like a form of gold-card health insurance. To exclude
disease carriers, foul winds from the east.

MY EVENING WALK, coming away from the halogen glow
of the glasshouse on Euston Road, its meetings, libraries
and collections, the great display of fetishes and medical
specimens, is illuminated by the faith that the city could
be rebuilt, the surplus of trade and acquired or inherited
wealth channelled for the public good. Samuel Pepys and
John Evelyn, friends and correspondents, devoted much
of their energy to plotting, designing and fitting out shelters and hospitals for distressed mariners and soldiers who
would otherwise face beggary on the unforgiving streets.

What entranced me, stepping just a few yards out of
my knowledge, and staying clear of Euston Road, was the
recovery of momentum, energy and stamina, in processing down streets with which I was unfamiliar, but which
appeared so self-confident, confirmed in their identity.

Endsleigh Gardens. Woburn Walk. Bow-fronted shops and the spidery footfall of W. B. Yeats and his visitors, the living and the dead. Seances and tea parties. Golden Dawn. Modest urban-village enterprises still hanging on: food, hair, newspapers. Bridal froth. Snack bar. A blue plaque for the novelist Dorothy Richardson, the early modernist of *Pilgrimage* fame. 'A novel,' they say, 'about the act of writing.' And then *Librairie du Maghreb*. A heaped book cave with damp cardboard boxes under flapping rain curtains. *Vous y trouverez l'introuvable.*

Burton Street. Burton Place. And Cartwright Gardens (formerly Burton Crescent). The name should have alerted me. Was this *James* Burton? The promoter of an East Sussex retirement colony? The one with a pyramidal tomb and a viewing slit? Burton pioneered a profession that combined architecture, rapacious development and the schmoozing necessary for acquiring parcels of land in the right places. Burton's residence at Tavistock House is now occupied by the British Medical Association. Beyond property speculation, Burton and his eldest son, William Ford, owned and managed gunpowder mills in Tunbridge.

Small hotels. Submarine lights in the portholes. Travellers, fresh from terminal stations, guard their luggage while they wait at unstaffed desks: one-night-only refugees. Here are hideaways for urgent assignations. A stopover crescent stocked with cabin-rooms providing very temporary respite. Already spotless pavements are being swept by migrant domestics taking the evening air and offering well-meant but useless advice to confused arrivals, who are prodding at their miniature phone maps.

On what had once been the sprawling Skinners Estate, I was charmed by a golden camel parked on a roof beside the Skinners Arms. An ill-favoured, east-facing beast waiting for Lawrence of Arabia? Or a drugged import soon to be skinned? I deciphered the black-on-white letters above the entrance to the narrow courtyard or service area of a mansion block: SINCLAIR HOUSE. But which Sinclair? A road not taken? Some unknown relative? After returning home, I checked the reference. 'The property you are looking for no longer exists.'

Sinclair House, Thanet Street, Bloomsbury. A good address. Noticed by contemporary developers, Sinclair House is glossed as being situated in a 'charming quiet road', a block serviced by a resident caretaker. Five minutes, as they always boast, from mainline railway stations, British Museum, British Library, university and hospital. 'Please prove that you are human by typing the text,' the website requires. 'Add your own contribution.'

A few moments of research gave me grounds for closer identification. Sinclair House sat squarely within the boundaries of an estate acquired by Sir Andrew Judd in the seventeenth century. The estate was presented to the Skinners' Livery Company, so that they could act as Trustees for the benefit of Tonbridge School. The portion on the south side of Euston Road, where I had paused on my walk, was once farmland, on which stood Bowling Green House and its pleasure grounds. In 1807, building leases were granted to James Burton, the architect responsible for the speculative, south-coast folly known as Burton St Leonard's – the twilight resort where I was now spending much of my time, escaping London. Streets in the Bloomsbury estate took their names from Kent and East Sussex: Tonbridge, Hastings, Thanet. By the middle of the nineteenth century, there were numerous houses of ill repute in the district, seventy of which were cleared in 1840. Some of the brothels were swiftly rebranded as boarding houses, awkward accommodation for workers or downwardly mobile clerks feeling the pinch. The arrival of Sinclair House, this redbrick monster, attracted a new demographic.

I circumambulated the behemoth from Hastings Street to Thanet Street. Entrances were camera-secure. There were numbered buttons for whisper-boxes. Strange that in

London's reprise of Burton's Hastings retirement colony, there should be another boat of a building, a dreadnought to set beside Marine Court in St Leonards, where we had our flat. On the far side of the building that fronted Sinclair House was a heritage plaque for the painter Paul Nash, another sometime man of the coast.

London estates take their time to bed in to the mulch. You can't track them, minute by minute, like some pre-disgraced politician on a flight from Nairobi to Heathrow. Or a vial of polonium-210 on a weekend mini-break from Moscow. Estates emerge, slowly and with subterfuge, from the grasp of a wealthy aristocrat wanting to secure family and position, or from some government initiative, the confidence (or desperation) to believe that there must be a better way. A better use for this land. Architects, planners, visionaries and investors draw up their dossiers. With the passing years, errors and accidents, the estate must grow into itself. Skinners Estate conserved its history without strain. The walker is permitted to experience, in the fading light of a late-winter afternoon, what was once here. In the custodianship of survival, there is a special tolerance for old pubs and cafés, *hotels de passe*, fenced gardens.

And then, somehow, out of nowhere, Argyle Walk: a cobbled post-historic passageway, an alley set with feathery, shivering trees against tall and sinister tenements. Hopeless drug deals are going down, crannies are found for shelter.

You will notice the invisibles, the ones who have been here from the start, the same faces, Victorian or Jacobean, in different rags: collateral damage of improvement schemes. They are swallowed by the shadows. Down on their luck and down on the stones. Too weak or disabused to beg. A single prostitute in a yellow faux-leather jacket hugs the corner, exposed in a pool of sour light and pecking red at a cigarette. She is watched, at a distance, by two pimps who might be her younger brothers, circling on stolen Boris bikes.

The path carries me to Vernon Rise, and uphill towards Percy Circus with the blue plaque for Vladimir Ilyich Lenin: the house where he stayed in 1905. After that familiar marker, I didn't need to think about where I was going: more estates, riper speculations, larger squares. You'll notice them in superior costume dramas like the 2017 BBC reprise of *Howard's End*. Islington is promoted to mythic Bloomsbury. You can admire the honoured possessions in these houses, all the books and paintings, the cultivated lives. Now I am overtaken by faster walkers and in-the-zone, horizon-eyed cyclists warming up for the towpath.

FURTHER

John Evelyn's Mulberry Tree

'Their demoralisation is catching. They not only pass on physical
disease, they infect us with their depression.'

Chris Petit, *Pale Horse Riding*

THEY CALLED IT THE PEPYS ESTATE to reference Samuel, the
great Restoration diarist, and his association with the Royal
Naval Dockyard. As Clerk to the Navy Board and Secretary
to the Admiralty, Pepys came frequently to Deptford, by
river, by coach – or the occasional marshy walk, reading
as he went, after being rowed across the Thames, from his
property in Seething Lane. Pepys was a man of interests,
one of the liveliest and most engaged of London citizens. He
was never inhibited about accepting the tributes that came
with office, but he did improve efficiency in the Navy Yards.
He trimmed the slack of accepted corruption and delivered
clean books of record. When charges were brought, political tides turning after the accession of James II, he
mounted a spirited defence of his position.

The Greater London Council showpiece development,
begun in 1966 and completed in 1969, was not named after
John Evelyn, the other (and much wordier) diarist of those
years, even though his own park at Sayes Court, inherited
from his wife's family, was the immediate neighbour of
the forty-five-acre site chosen for this experiment in public
housing. Evelyn has his busy street, his vestigial garden. But

something of the man's hauteur, his determination to live at a distance from the heat and pestilence of the City, made Pepys a choicer emblem for the new enterprise.

I walked to riverside Deptford on a cold Sunday morning in November, in order to meet two former tenants of Bence House on the Pepys Estate, the filmmaker Andrew Kötting and his daughter, Eden. I knew that this was where Eden had spent her first years. The low-rise flats and general environs were a hub of recollected pleasures: scents, tastes, sights, screams and embraces. This was the primal family home and the cave of Kötting's maturing imagination.

There was a leap of faith in attempting to set up home in an unknown and challenging environment. Andrew and his partner, Leila McMillan, were newly returned from a year venturing through Latin America. After a period of bedding down, in the delirium of that moment, wherever a corner could be found, so long as it was south of the river, the young couple were awarded a 'Hard to Let' council flat on the sixth floor of Bence House, on the Evelyn Road perimeter of this special-needs estate. Because that was, by reputation, its current status.

Andrew and Leila were artists, performers and hands-on manufacturers of difficult-to-promote objects and events. Leila stitched, sketched and welded. 'I'd completely forgotten how much fun we had,' Andrew said. Fun was the key to the domestic project, the loving alliance. Shared ambitions. Shared community. River. The flat agreed.

In their starter-home sanctuary, Andrew remembered covering the floor with rabbits. 'There was a scene in a film I made at the time,' he said, 'that involved me pulling a dozen tin Milagros from the end of my penis.' Milagros are compact 'miracle' charms, much favoured in Mexico and Peru. The tokens had been sourced by the Köttings on their travels. Milagros also function as ex-votos, as offerings made in the wake of a miraculous recovery.

The enamelled hearts pierced by fiery swords, the

paintings of chopped limbs I had inspected in the vitrines of the Euston Road collection, would be nailed to wooden representations of favoured saints. They might also be carried on difficult journeys, such as the helter-skelter peregrinations of Andrew and Leila through the sprawled cities, shacks, beaches, jungles, abandoned mining towns and mountain settlements of South America. On his return to Deptford, in the wake of so many other piratical voyagers, Kötting looked for rituals to animate the walls and floors and bricks and windows of the new flat.

Unread, William Blake's *A Descriptive Catalogue of Pictures, Poetical and Historical Inventions*, published in 1809, became Andrew's manual. 'The British Antiquities are now in the Artist's hands; all his visionary contemplations, relating to his own country and its ancient glory, when it was, as it again shall be, the source of learning and inspiration. And all the fables ... of the warlike naked Britons; of Merlin; of Arthur's conquest of the whole world; of his death, or sleep ... of the Druid monuments or temples; of the pavement of Watling Street; of London stone; of the caverns in Cornwall, Wales, Derbyshire; of the elemental beings called by us by the general name of fairies ... All these things are written in Eden.'

'WRITTEN IN EDEN.' And on Eden too. And by Eden. And through Eden. The daughter. And the idea. Eden Kötting ...

These were some of the stories Andrew told when we returned to Bence House, to stand between the estate car park and an ill-favoured play area. We took shelter in the lee of a sharp hedge. 'Everything began,' Andrew explained, pointing, 'in that bedroom.' The films, the book production, the performances and provocations. And Eden herself. And the full history was still there to be touched, behind the new cobalt window frame and the questionable cladding: intact, inviolate. Andrew made all his Deptford work 'in an attempt to cure a damaged leg, lung, heart, spleen,

'Everything began,' Andrew explained, pointing, 'in
that bedroom'. Bence House, Pepys Estate.

infertility'. The rituals of production were obvious exten-
sions of the scars of self-harm, willed or otherwise, on his
body. The blue-ink drawings on his ankles, a storyboard of
significant incidents.

BEFORE WE BEGIN OUR CIRCUIT of the Pepys Estate, Andrew
reads a quote from Gilles Ivain. He puffed steam into the
cold air as a grace note. 'All cities are geological; you cannot
take three steps without encountering ghosts bearing all the
prestige of their legends. We move within a *closed* landscape
whose landmarks constantly draw us towards the past.'

Eden, shivering but comfortable in her wheelchair, gar-
landed in a chaplet of wildflowers, a sturdy Ophelia rescued
from drowning, munches through a thick wad of petrol-
station sandwiches. She has a lusty appetite when it suits
her. A strong and contained young woman, happy, as she
indicates with Makaton hand signs and 'utterspeak' chirps,

to be back in this fondly remembered place with the great looming father-presence – 'Papapapa!' – to whom she is invisibly attached by all sorts of bonds. To be performing again! In costume! Green binoculars slung around her neck. Eden's fingernails, for this event, are painted as red as the poppies in her garland. As Andrew's gypsy neckerchief.

IN THE 2002 PROJECT known as *Mapping Perception*, undertaken with the neurophysiologist Dr Mark Lythgoe, Andrew filmed Eden brandishing those binoculars, as she stared through the darkness that was inside and the pinpricks of light on the distant horizon of an unfathomed world. Twinned tubes filled with smoke pressed against her innocent eyes. As her father set himself to scan 'numberless moments when I was not: the non-born'.

Kötting, Lythgoe and the other male participants in the brain-mapping project are photographed, dressed in seventeenth-century ruffs, re-enacting Rembrandt's *The Anatomy Lesson of Dr Nicolaes Tulp*. A macabre ceremony in which, on no firm evidence, Sebald places Sir Thomas Browne: 'who was engaging more profoundly with the mysteries of the human body than ever before.' Browne was certainly in Holland in 1632 when a petty thief was hanged and dissected by Tulp before the Guild of Surgeons. Sebald describes the performance as 'the harrowing of flesh'.

Meditating on this episode in his Norwich hospital bed, his vision still cloudy, senses numb, Sebald hears the rising and falling voices of two chattering nurses: 'a kind of warbling such as comes from the throats of birds, a perfect, fluting sound, part celestial and part of the song of the sirens.' This is Eden. This is the excited praise-song she makes. The chirruping of the child carried around the ragged fringes of Britain in Kötting's coastal odyssey film, *Gallivant*.

The Kötting men tower over the prone figure of the long-legged, thin-legged, bare-legged and very much alive

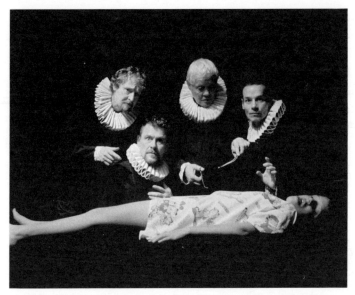

From *Mapping Perception*. Andrew Kötting's Anatomy Lesson.

Eden. Who, early in the game, learned to relish the demands of her father: play, collaborate, hug and laugh out loud. Grip those coloured pens. Make a new picture. 'Throughout the film making process,' said Dr Lythgoe, 'there was never an occasion that Eden wouldn't waddle through her home to sit in front of the video to look at herself after a day's filming.'

Andrew had succumbed to the right to buy – the family needed more space – sold up in Bence House, moved to the coast. But nothing tarnished the imprint of that fabled time. On so many other expeditions, the filmmaker invoked the Pepys Estate as a marker of integrity. This is what urban life should be. Love ignited here. Eden was born. That miracle. That impossible challenge. A strange gift, unwrapped and bloody, from the country of the unborn. He read everything he could lay his hands on to prove how little he was ever going to know, how his destiny had been changed forever. He ran the riverbank and the tunnel under it. He beat the bounds. He infiltrated the London Marathon and was exposed as an unlicensed finisher. They snatched back his complimentary Mars bar.

Eden was born in Guy's Hospital in 1988, after severe foetal distress, by emergency caesarean section. She was diagnosed with Joubert syndrome, a debilitating condition with a disconnect between her brain and the rest of her body. This was a rare heterogeneous genetic disorder causing vermis hypoplasia and other neurological complications. Manifestations include hypotonia, ataxia, psychomotor retardation, ocular-motor apraxia and neonatal respiratory abnormalities.

The parents, according to statements given at the time, were in a stable, six-year relationship and in occupation of a three-bedroom council flat. Health visitors were alerted. Andrew and Leila, better than most, were able to appreciate the intimate connection between the occulted design of the estate and the wellbeing of those who lived within its perimeter and protection. The verdict, the life sentence, arrived from somewhere else, an unexplained genetic tangle seeded over countless generations. The estate had no part in the fairy's gift of this condition or in its diagnosis, but it provided a secure, knowable territory in which social and medical responses could be tried and tested. In its modest way, Bence House was a blessing.

'Council estates have the effect of making people feel worse about themselves, and in turn, physically worse than other members of society,' Lynsey Hanley wrote in *Estates: An Intimate History* (2007). But, paradoxically, the Pepys Estate, after Eden's birth, after she was carried back to her first home, functioned very well as playpen and crèche. The medical centre offered support. There was still a functioning system in place. Eden progressed towards becoming herself, 'articulating through signing'.

'Today, she tells me of a dream,' Andrew recorded. 'A car breaks down and some dogs come out of the forest to mend it. The faster they lick, the quicker it goes. Her imagination has found a higher ground.' Andrew treasured lost Deptford days, 'surfing through this city underbelly'. The city responded. The city ignored his nuisance.

TODAY, AT THE START OF OUR WALK, raised voices bang and echo around the unruly dock of morning-after Bence House motors, German and Japanese, far newer and smarter than their warring owners. Families emerge, underdressed and unsorted, in a fashion somewhere between bedroom and street. The rubbish chute clatters. Andrew remembers how the council narrowed the apertures through which household junk could be posted, in order to prevent the disposal of inconvenient bodies (before they went off). The brief was to design a hole too small to take a human head. Ordinary domestic disputes that got out of hand, territorial drug wars brought indoors, could be neatly tidied away, Kötting implied, through the refinement of butchery by thinner slices. Bence House chutes told no tales.

The abuse, the ritual shouting and swearing, was affectionate, kept within pre-arranged limits. The woman gave it out. The kids waited beside the locked car. The man in the vest turned his back and walked away from the litany of insults, straight through the traffic to the off-licence. Car doors were slammed. Even when there was nobody left to receive her complaints, the woman sustained the pitch of her aria, the sum of the sins of the world. How it is. For women. And for her in particular. Wrong sex. Cruel fate.

'The privet hedges stop where the sounds of shirtless men shouting begins,' wrote Lynsey Hanley. Andrew Kötting arrived here from the land of privet hedges in deep suburbia around Chislehurst. He was, electively, one of nature's shirtless men. His bellows were largely comedic, part of the stage act, but also – on his own, at night, deep in the Pyrenean forest – genuine, soul-searing howls of pain.

The outfit Andrew has assembled for pushing his twenty-nine-year-old daughter over the bumps and kerbs at pace, with no moans, is horse-trader. Hairy grey tweed with scarlet trim. Close-buttoned, mid-calf coat. Sporty red neckerchief. Three-day sandpaper stubble. Silver-mirrored dark glasses. Eden chortles, enjoys the rush. The possibility of being tipped out. NO FLY TIPPING. 'Arright, John?'

But John is not all right. John is not happy at all. Sir John Betjeman gave the Pepys Estate the thumbs down. From a great height. A helicopter-spotter lining up the whole concrete flood plain of the Deptford estate – 'sometimes they called them towers' – for demolition by friendly bombs when they had done with Slough.

1969. *An Englishman's Home.* A documentary in the *Bird's-Eye View* series produced by Edward Mirzoeff to put a varnished frame around country piles and to scorn 'car port' estates for plastics reps. With atonal bleeps reserved for those unfortunates from terraced streets unhoused by war: 'out of the devastation, slabs arose'. Hitler's shadow-casting bomber squadrons tracked the serpentine Thames to pave the way for the misguided disciples of Le Corbusier.

It was once a requirement for late modernists to sneer at Betjeman, but the tide began to turn long before the manifest horrors of Grenfell Tower revealed municipal short-termism verging on criminality. Conservative commentators took Sir John's Deptford anathemas as prescient. 'It can't be right.' The helicopter caresses the crude geological stacks of the Pepys Estate in a mating dance. 'Where can the heart be that sends a family to the twentieth floor in such a slab as this? It can't be right, however fine the view.' The lifts don't work. Neighbours are strangers. The tenants are prisoners of state benevolence. Are the children safe down below?

'When brutalist monstrosities such as Grenfell Tower first started popping up all over London ... poet John Betjeman was a vocal and tireless critic of this brave new world ... Re-reading some of his lines on the subject, he sounds more like a doomed prophet,' wrote Fiorella Nash in *The*

Catholic World Report (16 June 2017).

The Betjeman argument, given weight by pinched budgets, failing services, shortages of caretakers and maintenance staff, and lethal fudges in renovation, was challenged by the experience of the Pepys Estate, as reported by Andrew Kötting and others. Despite the obvious flaws, the practical difficulties of caring for Eden, transporting her to health centres and to special school, Andrew was enraptured by locality. He loved the mess.

It was left to Lynsey Hanley to give the twist to Betjeman. 'Council houses were never intended to be holding cages for the poor and disenfranchised,' she said, 'but somehow, that's how they've ended up.'

For Andrew Kötting, those Deptford years were a paradise lost. 'The flat. Red brick, yellow insides,' he said. 'An entrance to the rear. Puddled with piss in summertime and blocked with adolescent bliss in wintertime. The lift gleams with spittle, the corridors with polish. Up to the sixth floor, the corridor, second on the left and in. Home, their home. Good-to-be-home, home. Bence House, Pepys Estate, home.'

When the filmmaker came to layer a soundtrack for *Gallivant* in 1996, he chose to sample the voice of Betjeman from *An Englishman's Home* for a sequence tracking past seaside bungalows at Pevensey Bay.

WE HEAD TOWARDS THE RIVER, Andrew pushing with one hand, gesturing with the other. Eden's green binoculars penetrate the smokescreen of regeneration. With her painted nails, she reaches for her father's hand. They *know* this hedged corner, our temporary shelter from the wind. The designated play area was ignored by kids back in the day and is quite deserted now. Ground-floor flats were always favoured by dealers, Andrew reckoned. Easy come and go. He chose to park his van at a safe distance in a lock-up. The Transit was stacked with finds for the market stall, with electrical cables and potentially saleable lumps stripped from industrial ruins: cash money from local no-questions-asked scrapyards. Andrew's punkish performance group, Being Karnal, celebrated Deptford in their 1982 anthem: 'Mine is a place of faded grey, mine is a place to pass away. Cement the land.'

The prospectus for the original Pepys Estate included elevated walkways, streets in the sky that connected the separate blocks. You would never need to set your foot on suspect ground, thereby suppressing race memories of impenetrable marshland and pressgangs charged with supplying the navy with unwilling hands. The walkway bridges are broken. The corridors bricked up. Utopian theories have been aborted by the practicalities of crime prevention. Odours are triggers. Andrew lists: verges sour with cat piss, the earthy slush of sodden leaves, bacon burning in the pan, the grunting blokeish sweat of the man-gym, wet paper pulp rotting in mounds, kebab on the spin. 'The lovely smell of the place,' he says. 'The heat and the pace of days that are gone. Spicy West African voices.'

He is channelling a state of mind that Aristotle called 'Entelechia'. He wants to capture the essence of the soul of the place: *the soul's estate*. 'The balsame of our memories,' said Sir Thomas Browne. 'In eternitie there is no distinction of Tenses.' The Norwich doctor spurned predestination in favour of the Almighty's unchallenged 'determination of our estates to come'.

And come they did: low-rise blocks and stand-apart towers, some of them now taken out of the public realm, revamped and floated on the free market. Kötting shows off remnants of maritime architecture: ceremonial gateways, colonnades, officers' quarters and storage vaults. They are touched by the prestige of documented history. And in the safe hands of new investors.

Earl Mountbatten, the last Viceroy of India, was invited downriver to declare the Pepys Estate open on 13 July 1966.

Victualling Yard, Pepys Estate.

He made it known that every tenant should be supplied, free
of charge, with a printed legend of the naval dockyard. Let
them understand how fortunate they are to be lodged on
hallowed ground. The estate was, he suggested, a battleship
in dry dock. The connected royal, a pro-consul staggering
under the weight of honours, had a rather peculiar sense
of his role. This was not a social experiment but a colony.

What is left of all that? Wind-tossed spaces with puddles
of remembered green. Odd buildings dedicated to health
and recreation. There is a youth club with a pointy roof
supposed to reference a Kentish oast house. The stone skull
of a cow marks the point of access to the former Victualling Yard: bully beef and maggots! A flagstone esplanade,
a rampart between towers, gives Andrew the opportunity
to engage in banter with a group of estate girls who are
hanging out. And interested to meet Eden. Who is both a
young woman and a sort of child.

In its earliest days, Pepys Estate was almost exclusively

Completed in the mid sixties, the three newly-built Pepys
Estate towers were amongst the tallest in London.

white. It was supposed to accept the Mountbatten prescription and behave like an outpost of empire reluctantly ceded
to the sullen natives. A rock against further alien invasion.
A Cockney Gibraltar without the Barbary apes swinging
from the balconies.

WE COME AT LAST TO THE RIVER, to Aragon Tower. Could
we have arrived by accident at a lighthouse dedicated to
the Surrealists? A thrusting psychogeographical memorial
to the poet Louis Aragon, author of *Paris Peasant*, an influential work of urban drifting? Merlin Coverley, in his guide
to *Psychogeography* published in 2006, claims that *Paris
Peasant* 'introduces an element of political protest that first
recognises the future role of the urban wanderer, as the
detached observer is forced to face up to the destruction of
the city and to engage in the struggle against it.'

Aragon Tower is its homonym, Arrogance Tower. A

twenty-nine-floor blue-sky mosaic with pyramidical steps at the distant summit. The tower is residential, privately owned, and has fourteen penthouse units. It has been described, inevitably, as the catalyst for the regeneration of the Deptford riverbank. Sculptural heads, in the English tradition of disembowelled traitors, or pirates chained and left to the tide before being decapitated, have been displayed around the river-facing base of the tower. They are protected behind a locked gate, so that Thames Path casuals have no chance of reading the plaque identifying the faces, the ones framed as a 'Wall of Ancestors'. The sculptor responsible is Martin Bond, a local man, former classical pianist and illegal immigrant. Bond made the crossing from Mexico into the USA, to play with a punk band in Baltimore.

The arrangement of the worthies on Aragon Tower, friends of the artist interspersed with an eclectic selection of notables loosely associated with the area, has been changed. With Eden's green binoculars, you can identify Grinling Gibbons, the woodcarver who lodged in a cottage in the grounds of John Evelyn's Sayes Court. And Peter the Great, a less disciplined Evelyn tenant: premature bad-behaviour super-oligarch with a taste for drunken orgies, setting fire to the furniture and pushing guests around the formal gardens in a wheelbarrow. Olaudah Equiano, the author and abolitionist, enslaved, brought to Deptford, sold again: he's on the wall too. Francis Drake, criminous sea captain and circumnavigator, knighted near this spot. Elizabeth the First, who was rowed downriver to do the deed. And Catherine of Aragon, Henry VIII's deposed queen, the Spanish lady who gifted her name to the tower. Hard to decide now if these are life masks of the noisy dead or death masks of the almost living: chalky after-images of the recently expelled.

The major developers Berkeley Homes (East Thames) snatched the jewel of the Pepys Estate from Lewisham Council. The riverfront is no longer available to council tenants. It is a means-tested promenade based on an abdication of sensibility. Three towers: Aragon, Eddystone and Daubeny. Beacons of reflected light divorced from navigation. The broad river scintillates, a succession of prismatic incidents. Water has copious flow, but no time.

The last man left standing in Aragon Tower was Lez Brookes. He traded as 'Pocket the Juggling Clown', a children's entertainer. Lez, who had lived in the tower for twenty years, alone at the end, while he waited for the inevitable expulsion, patrolled the deserted corridors on his unicycle like the child from *The Shining* grown old and feral. Manky Deptford pigeons fluttered in and out of broken windows. The council, growing impatient, cut off heat and water, but the clown had taken advantage of Thatcher's 'Right to Buy' scheme. He believed that the property he had purchased was his to sell at a time of his own choosing. He was the wrong demographic. A stilt-walker with the tallest stilts in London. And an audience of drill-wielding hard hats.

The TV set in the last flat is dead, cables sliced, but hustling crews turn up to feature his story. The deal was already done and dusted, Lewisham Council trousered £10 million from Berkeley Homes. The pitch being that new money will inevitably bring coffee outlets and big-window gyms into the area, as indeed it has: if not for the benefit of the locally decanted. The expensive facilities are for incomers, thirsty Lycra cyclists and joggers.

At the finish, the solitary clown acknowledged that he had made a 'killing'. He picked up £180,000 for the flat he'd bought for £50,000. And which would now trade for around half-a-million quid. In the lifestyle TV series shot in the relaunched Aragon Tower, champagne corks pop. Innocent investors have no idea where they really are. Like Betjeman, they swoon over the view. And it is all theirs, they own the wide sky. 'Communities will naturally integrate,' say the planners. The view-collectors drink to that. The

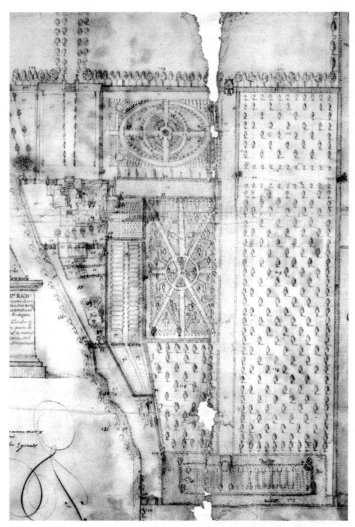

John Evelyn's drawing of his garden at Sayes Court, 1653.

new lifts work. The building is secure. The masks on the exterior wall are giving nothing away.

WHO YOU WALK WITH alters what you see. I was conscious that my ramble around the Pepys Estate was little more than an extended portrait of Andrew and Eden. Buildings played no part in Eden's condition, but the atmosphere of the estate and the allied river did provide a nurturing element. Notes from the walk transcribed, I had to make a late-afternoon drift on my own terms, looking again at some of the places brushed against on Andrew's conducted tour.

In Pepys Park, I met a ninety-year-old woman, horse-shoe-spined, doubled over a stick, pushing through the leaves as if they were rubble and calling plaintively after a ratty dog on an extendable lead. 'Bella. Bellabella*bella*.' The distance marker said that it was 115 miles to Dover.

They hadn't, as yet, locked up for the night. I had found the thing I didn't know I was looking for: Sayes Court, the 'lost garden' of the diarist John Evelyn. And if the tenuous connection with Pepys, by way of the Naval Yard, pro-vided a convenient heritage identity for the estate where Eden Kötting spent her first years, Evelyn's park had been allowed to remain a tolerated lacuna, a shaded walk. I had no expectation of seeing it again. The beds swallowed light.

I hadn't progressed twenty yards before I experienced the way that, after trudging an unspecified number of miles, burdened with accretions of detail, the walker is submerged in the walk. In the context of this Deptford expedition, I attributed the effect to my prolonged contemplation of Eden's privileged condition, somewhere between mundane reality and the dream of talking animals licking cars. Being part-born, part of this other world, the older place, made her an oracle for the territory. Or that was what we pro-jected on to her. In just the way I needed to dignify my arbitrary changes of direction, my truffling, by calling on the authority of Sir Thomas Browne.

Browne was charmed by *flos maris*, a stain floating across the surface of the sea; a substance, derived from the sperm whale, that was not seminal, nor the kind of amniotic leakage in which some strange Caliban creature might evolve, to emerge among the derelict docks. A primitive pub-sign portrait made into flesh. Should Browne's mysterious substance burn like the oil in the table lamps of old London by which other writers scratched out their tales?

Evelyn made an entry in his diary for 3 June 1658: 'A large whale has been taken betwixt my land butting on the Thames and Greenwich, which drew an infinite concourse to see it … After a long conflict it was killed with a harping yron, struck in the head, out of which it spouted blood … by two tunnels, and after a horrid grone it ran quite on shore and died. Its length was fifty-eight foote, height sixteen, black skin'd like coach-leather, very small eyes, great taile, and onely two small finns, a pickled snout, and a mouth so wide that divers men might have stood upright in it; no teeth, but suck'd the slime onely as thro' a grate of … whale-bone, the throate yet so narrow as would not have admitted the least of fishes … '

Sayes Court Park was a dirty mosaic of red and gold. Brick walls and recent fences screened the enclosure. Evelyn's Deptford affiliations have been left to a bleak parade of shops where a smacked-out Goth with wild staring eyes has been spray-painted on a set of roll-down shutters alongside graffito for LAST DAYS OF ROME. The local landowner's tribute consists of a grey execution block with his name and dates, into which has been inserted a giant metal feather, a quill pen to keep the diary running into eternity – if anyone is willing to pull it out. Several have tried, and left their fingerprints, without success.

But you can try too hard. Sayes Court never reached the foreshore of the Thames. Evelyn inherited the house and gardens from his father-in-law, Richard Brown. A notable horticulturalist and author of essays on gardens, trees and planting, the great diarist envisioned his beds and parterres like the unfulfilled painter he was fated to be.

I was about to return to the busy main road, to Evelyn Street, when I came on the mulberry tree. A gnarled but slender trunk supporting a tangle of branches, some low to the ground, swallowed in the darkening sky like a spill of ink on quality paper. The solitary tree was a map of absence. There was nothing here of the bountiful mulberry plantation at St James' Palace, where Samuel Pepys, overcome by heady scents and the proximity of royalty, sported and groped.

The story is told of the wrong kind of mulberries, black saplings, imported by James I, in order to foster an English silk industry. Scholars dispute the provenance. This fenced off and labelled Deptford tree is perhaps a third generation descendant of the original sapling, planted under instruction from Evelyn or his father-in-law. The black mulberry, according to the Oxford plant scientist Barrie Juniper, is 'wildly polyploid': sterile and unable to reproduce from seed.

Discussing the matter with Andrew Honey, the Bodleian Library's conservation and collection officer, Juniper discovered that saplings had been cultivated from black berries gathered in Sayes Court Park. One of the saplings on his low-lying Oxford allotment perished in the recent floods, the survivor is struggling.

Evelyn's caged mulberry still manages to crop heavily with dark blood-berries. The tree's life force is sustained by shadows from abandoned riverside warehouses and the febrile heat of regeneration projects. Once again it appears that homeopathic doses of pollution are what give us the strength to carry on. To lay out, in the teeth of the evidence, our paradise gardens and utopian estates.

Golden Lane

'O Rose, thou art sick!'
William Blake

TENNIS COURTS HAVE BEEN LAID over the former bowling green. Less maintenance. A new demographic. This is no country for old men. Different sounds. *Shot!* The tasteful grey-blue twin rectangles, nicely kept, no high mesh fences with cut links, no barbecued benches and drug wraps, have been given ash-pink borders, so that the whole effect – if the players, the enthusiastic, self-umpiring, Sunday morning mixed doubles, are airbrushed from the scene – is calculated but attractive, like an architect's drawing for a utopia that will never have to be delivered.

Except that, as I now discovered, the Golden Lane Estate, secure within its own rectangle, between Baltic Street, Golden Lane, Fann Street and Goswell Road, *was* delivered in 1957. By Chamberlin, Powell & Bon, an enlightened firm of architects, former lecturers and Le Corbusier enthusiasts from Kingston School of Art. Conceived, approved, achieved. And still thriving. Or so it appeared at the conclusion of my tour.

The tennis players were colour coded, multicultural, and easy moving in unbranded and inoffensive leisurewear. Their confident calls and non-aggressive thumps – patpatpat*thwap*patpat*shot*! – offered a clip of unwitnessed

Golden Lane Estate as seen from the Goswell Road.

theatre to the surrounding, low-rise flats with their balconies like private boxes, proud among pink verticals picking
up on the strips dividing the two courts, as the smoky blues
and greys of the brickwork echo the playing surfaces with
their legible white lines and fresh white trim at the top of
the net. The former bowling club, sheltered from the street,
but on view to the City workers who had been the first
tenants, made way for this louder, faster, post-millennial
recreation, so much enjoyed by newcomers of varied free-
lance occupations, united by a sense of pride in the privilege
of belonging.

By 2016, 52 per cent of the flats on the Golden Lane
Estate had been sold on long leases under the 'Right to Buy'
scheme championed by Margaret Thatcher. The quality
of the original build, functional but idealistic, was much
appreciated by 'design conscious' investors. Prices now
reflected both the legend of a settled community and the
convenience of a location close to the City: the buzz of bars
and clubs around Smithfield and the concrete brutalism of
big brother Barbican, the subsequent development awarded

to Chamberlin, Powell & Bon by City planners delighted by positive critical responses to what had already been delivered on Golden Lane. Brutalism was coming back into fashion. Brutalism was a book – and an exhibition nested inside occupied exhibits you were free to stroll around and explore. There is nowhere better in London to get lost than the Barbican walkways, the dead ends, suspect corridors and stairs leading to brass-handled barriers like the doors of bullion safes.

TWO UNHURRIED LANE-SWIMMERS were taking advantage of the pool reserved for the fortunate denizens of the estate. Their safety was assured by the presence of a lifeguard on a high perch. But that word 'denizen' had been subverted: Geoffry Powell's vision of a sustainable urban life was threatened by a looming shadow on the southern horizon, in the conflicted space between the two familial estates, Golden Lane and Barbican. *The Denizen* (definite article) was a land grab sanctioned by the Darwinian rapaciousness and clubbable gangsterism of the City. Excess money, sick of its unlaundered bad-rep McMafia status, thirsts after solidity and substance. After *visible* monuments flattered by copywriters. Shrouded stacks hide behind screens of fantastic CGI boasts and fences sprayed like fake forests. Promises are never kept. Promises promise nothing. That is understood. The Denizen would provoke horrified resistance from the occupants of Bowater House on the southern border of the estate: their modest ration of London light (and peace of mind) stolen by the demolition of Bernard Morgan House, a police dormitory flattened to make way for another Taylor Wimpey development, high-spec show-flats for non-occupying occupiers and compliant investors.

But these property dramas, happening everywhere, are never as simple as they appear in blogs and impassioned broadsheet articles. On Fann Street we have the rather disconcerting spectacle of a vanishing section house for 110

City policemen, a militant group with their own rules and entitlements, their surveillance operations and rings of steel, being replaced by ninety-nine flats for civilians from all parts of the globe – and that act being challenged by the banners of a loose collective of name artists, counter-culturalists, curators and theoreticians. Writers who, in the recent past, had made capital out of their interactions with City police (unsanctioned photographers, urban exploration crews), were now presenting the expelled lodgers of Bernard Morgan House as yeoman Londoners like the original occupants of the Golden Lane Estate that arose from the ruins of the Blitz. The sleeping policemen acquired virtue by accidental association with the 'much loved' tiles of Bernard Morgan House. The threatened fabric glowed beneath its plastic cerements, its all-enveloping rain cape. Designed by J. Inness Elliott, and constructed in 1960, the section house was saluted by supporters of the Bowater House protest as a 'non-designated heritage asset'. The police shared their space, their canteen, shelter and warmth, with nurses. Here were two important service groups now diminished by government cuts and a management culture of manipulated statistics, the spinning of disaster.

I heard from a film editor, living in Bowater House, how she had waited months for the results of a PET (Positron Emission Tomography) scan on her young son, who was coping very well with the absences and grand mal seizures of epilepsy, at a time when important school exams were looming. She told me that there was just *one* PA, vital for the day-to-day running of a hospital department, answering phones, responding to emails and letters, allocated to five overstretched neurologists.

What is in question, in terms of our true heritage, is the status of the word *denizen*: 'an inhabitant, resident, an alien admitted to residence, anything adapted to a new place, an animal or plant not indigenous but successfully naturalized.' The suggestion in the air, as the residents of

Bowater House look fearfully across Fann Street at the emerging Taylor Wimpey stack, after being instructed that they should strike off their balconies if they want more light, is that this new development belongs in a special bardo, a refuge for future invisibles, those disembodied entities perching on the edge of an ill-defined boundary between heritage Cripplegate and a shiny reservation of space-pods independent of the topography that contains them. An estate, in the end, is that which is worthy of being marked on the map: an oasis charmed against rude incursions. The private made public and then privatised again.

I CAME TO GOLDEN LANE, never quite sure when I was trespassing, to contemplate the way this estate hovered between its original council origins and its present occupation by artists, writers, lawyers, architects, work-at-home laptop freelancers, and aging veterans of the earlier regime (tolerant of the newcomers and prepared, on occasion, to be quoted as part of the fabric).

On one of those darkening afternoons, I might find Chris Petit, author and filmmaker, taking an hour away from his desk, out on the tennis court in tracksuit bottoms, released from the dark trilogy on which he was working. His research was wide ranging. He trawled forgotten fictions, mounds of memoirs, documentary reports and unreliable autobiographies (ghosted or dictated) by war criminals who had dodged the noose. He escaped for road trips, as a fugue or reverie in which to disguise narrative threads that were becoming too visible or too obvious. The bleaker the terrain the better. Petit drove through the night to places many would prefer to avoid. Bunkers. Abandoned holiday camps. Retail parks. Railway hotels. Poland. The Baltic.

The filmmaker's particular vision of what an estate could become evolved through long hours battened down in Golden Lane, cramps and back spasms relieved by remedial sessions of tennis on that quiet court surrounded by blocks of occupied flats showing few signs of the life within. The percussive ritual – patpatpat*thwap*sorrypat*thwap* – was a secret ceremony, laying down a soundtrack against the grinding of the demolition crew, the evil dust. The estate was an organism in which each cell played its part, being in the City and of the City, but somehow distinct and separate.

Golden Lane had come into being through a firmly held conviction about what an estate should be: nothing of the pastiched, faux-ruralist village with its hierarchies, its paranoia over the wrong sort of aliens; no residue of the garden city as an off-highway, Arts and Crafts gulag of 'low-density monotony', neither city nor country. Bowater House, rescued from war damage, was self-sufficient and respectful of the territory in which it found itself. The architects drew on Le Corbusier or borrowed from his practice whatever they needed. Whatever could be smuggled across the borders of prejudice. Crescent House echoed Maisons Jaoul at Neuilly-sur-Seine, while the maisonettes that I visited, with their open-plan stairs, were reminiscent of l'Unité d'habitation in Marseille, but more modest.

Instead of looking out on parkland, the sea, the spectacle of life in the city, Bowater House, hung with banners of protest, faced a shrouded construction site, intrusive scaffolding and crews in hard hats. Chamberlin, Powell & Bon promoted Le Corbusier's notion of the estate as a microcosm, one segment of a radiant city.

Jonathan Meades, informed Europhile author, painter, cook, photographer (etc. etc.), was a friend and sometime colleague of Petit and his wife, Emma Matthews. He found significant virtue in aspects of concrete brutalism and leant his voice in support of the Golden Lane campaign against the demolition of Bernard Morgan House.

'While there can be no doubt that cities benefit from near-anarchic heterogeneity there can equally be no doubt that the combination of an officially sanctioned, Croesus inspired, near-anarchy has only the most baleful consequences. At

Protest banners, Bowater House.

some point the City of London's shiny, ostentatious self-destruction must stop ... Developers and architects have been subjected to only the frailest checks. The very idea of aesthetic control seems laughably quaint, a hangover from an age that valued propriety. Bernard Morgan House belongs to such an age. It is over fifty years old. Thus it has enjoyed what, by current measures, is an exceptional longevity ... Black bricks, knapped flints, concrete. Whilst the form may derive from Le Corbusier, the materials, unusual in this conjunction, derive from the industrial vernacular of the nineteenth century and the immemorial structures of the flint-constellated chalklands of the Thames Basin.'

Meades left London some years ago. After one false start, he now lives in Marseille, an apartment in Le Corbusier's l'Unité d'habitation.

THE MAISONETTES OF BOWATER HOUSE, presently an exhibition of banners challenging the emerging Taylor Wimpey stack, were conceived as suitable habitation for City caretakers, maintenance men, security operatives, and for nurses; the unseen army of workers on whom the commuting financiers and traders depended. The units were cleverly designed to maximise space and light. And as such they appealed to a new demographic, the ones who were copywriting the slogans for the protest banners.

ONE DAY WILL/ THIS SHADOW FALL. ALL THAT IS AIR/ MELTS INTO SOLID. PARASITES WILL STARVE IN/ THIS CARCASS OF CULTURE. CHILDREN NEED/ SUNLIGHT TO GROW. FREE EXORCISM WITH EVERY/ TAYLOR WIMPEY GHOST HOME. ZOMBIE INVESTORS/ TAKE STOCK.

They flap and fold in the wind like gaudy wrappings on a cake left out in the rain: decorative, jaunty and wounded. Indignant, aggrieved. That the malign shadow falls across *their* windows, across *their* tables and desks. Across, when the sun's beatitude obeys its lowest arc, Fortune Street Park: the benches and the tray-sized vegetable beds 'looked after by children from Prior Weston Garden Club'. And that slender American sweetgum tree with its star-shaped leaves, the one planted on 14 July in 2003 by Leo Chapman Esq., as a symbol of 'EC1 New Deal for Communities.'

The neighbourhood park, not much more than the length of a modest suburban garden, was the site where the community defined itself, where the children of the estate gathered to play, and where working mothers, taking a breather, found time to listen to the grandmothers, the old ones who were part of the foundation estate.

In their maisonettes, warmed by the sun's passage in winter, cooled by the shadows of the overhanging balconies in summer, they were nurtured by a confirmation of what it meant to belong to the working city, attentive to present difficulties and backstory: the Huguenot feather traders, the Welsh Church, the Elizabethan theatres.

Antonio Muñoz Molina, in his novel *Like a Fading Shadow*, is sensitised to an almost neurotic degree by those periods, like absences or seizures, in which the urban watcher becomes aware of plurality, the overlapping tidal convulsions of pedestrians: 'a benevolent flood of light, the sudden memory of the city.' Muñoz Molina has a base narrative tracking the period when James Earl Ray, Martin Luther King's fugitive assassin, hides in Lisbon, putting on time, accumulating newspapers, visiting prostitutes, as he explores the fantasy of escape to Africa. He is already a prisoner, fate in temporary remission, as he waits for the sickness to arrive.

He gobbles painkillers. He is febrile, sweating, walking endlessly around the docks and the steep streets. Alongside this documented and mythologised story, converted into numerous aborted fictions by the self-incarcerated assassin, Muñoz Molina folds in his own expeditions to Lisbon: as a young man with notebook and camera – and then, once more, as a successful author.

'Stories end,' he says, 'by disintegrating into others, dispersing, unravelling loose threads without a clear plot that intertwines with other stories and ends up travelling far from their starting point … flowing like rivers, without a sequence or beginning or end.'

I recognised the syndrome. This was exactly what was happening to me. Solid ground disappears from beneath tired feet. Stephen Greenblatt and Ramie Targoff catch the mood in their introduction to Sir Thomas Browne: 'He knew that a man who one day looked perfectly healthy could the next succumb to a fatal illness; that seemingly robust children would abruptly sicken and die; that people could scream with conviction that someone was sticking a pin in their flesh, when in fact the pain's source was entirely internal … There was nothing strange or uncanny about sickness or death.'

Finding shelter, no easy matter in our stretched city, is no guarantee of comfort and wellbeing. A fixed habitation anticipates stress, debt, and the spectre of compulsive, mindless improvement, with 'regeneration' as an incipient threat (the envelope on the mat): blocked highways, gaping holes, confrontation. Hospitals justify their crippling budgets by making us sick. 'Being healthy,' said Muñoz Molina, 'was like being right-wing.'

And it was true. I experienced, coming to Golden Lane Estate, an obscure underlay of guilt: that I was in reasonable health, free to wander, commissioned to comment. I had not, as yet, found my sickness vocation. It was coming, for sure, but I had not received official confirmation about the form it would take.

THE BOWATER HOUSE MAISONETTE occupied by Emma Matthews and her son, Louis, is heaped with archival boxes, films, hours of cultural retrievals: like the entire memory of an era when public broadcasting found the budget to keep a record of what was happening, and where, and why – and how the reforgotten and almost-known, illuminati, addicts, jazzmen, prophets and poets could be tracked to their lairs. It felt as if the duty of preserving cultural memory had fallen on this nuclear family. A frail raft holding out against the know-nothing, value-nothing futurism represented by Taylor Wimpey. One of the ironic consequences of the development process, Matthews told me, was that property values in Bowater House would be increased by the addition of their hollow neighbour with its glitz and swagger. A mute outrider of an emerging secret kept under wraps.

New technologies meant that Emma's editing tasks could be managed in a space under the stairs, on the table where meals were served, homework spread out, games played, paintings begun. Units designed for the essential labourers of the City – couples permitted, families rare – were attractive to professionals with the means to live like artisans of the new economy, on the edge of the action: Old Street's silicon roundabout, arts bureaucracy at the Barbican or the Museum of London, Bloomsbury publishers and bookshops and event organisers.

Louis Petit, whenever he was around, returned from school, heading out for tennis coaching, was a boy with considerable natural charm. Children, not subject to the endless debates and discussions of exhausted adults, are a better register for how well an environment functions. They make the best of what they are given and where they find themselves – if circumstances do not become, as they often must, too oppressive. Golden Lane still functioned. It functioned in its individual units and as a totality, an estate.

If there appeared, to the outsider, to be a high incidence of brain sickness, cabin fevers and neurological disorders, this should not be credited to the stress of the Denizen development. Some of the people I talked to on my circuit of the estate mentioned the funnel of pollution that was Beech Street, a blur of hustling traffic dividing the Barbican from Golden Lane. They blamed insults to lungs, badly wired nervous systems and faulty synapses, on a cocktail of soured air, the filth they were obliged to navigate. Mention was made of microscopic plastic granules in the comfort bottles of water they carried everywhere, as advised, for protection against being trapped on failing public transport or caught between coffee stops.

Long hours concentrating on detail on a small screen, running and re-running footage to find a rhythm, can't have helped. Emma Matthews suffered from crippling migraines. In editing, nothing is final (until it is); everything shifts, revives, excites, falls apart, begins again. A door opens two frames too late and the ninety-minute construct crashes. Start over from the beginning. But there is no beginning. You can run the newsreel backwards and the demolished station house rises proud from the dust. Smoke twists back into the bottle. Pathogens make different patterns. The disease of the city is in remission. We rub our knuckles against the bricks to be sure that we are still alive.

As the older commissioning processes collapsed, so the product was more open, deadlines were more flexible (who cares now?). There was no approved script on which to fall back. These were the years of yoga for the stiff neck, catalogue trawls for the ideal chair – black, German, orthopaedic – for the pressured spine: a never-ending quest for relief. Temporomandibular joint and muscle disorders. Questionable posture. Derangement of fractal image gardens. Shudder of manipulated sound. The quacks and healers and gong-tapping shamen suggest: massage, electronic devices, podiatry, dentistry (night grinding), regular morning exercise. Walk the river, run the park, buy a dog, swim the chlorine carpet. But the symptoms persist, storm warnings of angelic auras and hurting light before the next bout of sickness and prostration. The editor left prone, in pulsing darkness. The computer screen stalled, blotting up infinite projections of interior constellations.

There was a possible hereditary link, so researchers at Columbia University Medical Centre surmised, between migraine susceptibility and epilepsy: a 'co-morbidity'. But no firm data emerged from initial studies. 'Dizziness, ringing in the ears, zigzag lines and flashing lights, excess excitability in the brain.' Like epilepsy. And sometimes traceable along the branches of the family tree. Like the residue of a past vision, an episode on the road to Damascus, brought to violent and involuntary recall. The primal dream invading the bodily vessel of present occupation.

As well as demonstrating a flair for sketching and image making, Louis Petit had a part to play, as performer and journal keeper, in his father's road film, *Content*. And so he was. Or so he always struck me: notably contained, engaged, occupied. *Present*. Content in his own space, his special environment. Louis was also a promising tennis player, taking advantage of the Golden Lane facility, exploiting topspin and style to make up for lack of inches.

And then the seizures struck. Emma, looking back, thinks that there were early warning signs, minor absences. Moments when Louis was elsewhere. The syndrome manifested in the Bowater House flat, against the threat of stolen light, the battles with developers, but there was no hard evidence of cause and effect. The convulsions were not a protest against tensions over the quality of their future life.

The first grand mal seizure happened in February 2016. Sometimes there were a number of episodes in a single week. It was difficult, and very demanding, to get a diagnosis. Life becomes mired in the processes of hospital bureaucracy, travel and waiting. And more waiting. Louis had to be accompanied on his journey to school and on his return. Here was a contemporary variant of the feared 'falling sickness' that led to incarceration in the first Bethlehem Hospital, close to the Roman wall. Patients disappeared from the record, those who had no family or friends to support them in their trouble.

Eventually, arriving at Great Ormond Street, Emma was advised to try Louis with a new diet. 'It is completely full time,' she told me, 'working out meals and preparing them. They've got to be exactly measured to the gram, each ingredient. The fats, carbs and proteins have to balance to produce ketones rather than glucose as fuel for the brain.'

The diet did help. Louis was free of seizures for about six weeks. Emma's life was changed in ways I could never have imagined. When she practised, full time, as an editor, with that intensity of concentration, she seemed to live on chocolate biscuits, coffee, mugs of tea. She rarely cooked.

Bowater House days were restructured around the meticulous, almost alchemical preparation and production of meals for Louis – which Emma shared, with minor variants, the addition of potatoes for example. Amiable sauntering was off the menu. Beyond the personal drama of her son's condition and the steps she took to alleviate it, life running on, school, editing projects, shopping, there was the unyielding assault on her immediate surroundings. It was right outside her window, those hard-hat

Emma and Louis Petit by Katherine Fawssett.

spectators, resting on their high scaffold, looking in. The
war for light.

Emma fired off emails. She gave lucid, embattled television interviews. She blogged and telephoned and made
notes for legal challenges. She championed collective resistance and she disputed the treatments offered to her son. She
had become, by force of circumstance, the Rosa Luxem-
burg of Golden Lane. Her energies, in the face of this daily
grind, were astonishing.

There is a strikingly elegant portrait of Emma and
Louis, together on the sofa, taken by Katherine Fawssett
for a campaigning piece in the *Mirror*. The concern, this
time, is very familiar to the estates I encountered in the
Lower Lea Valley at the time of the great Olympic enclo-
sures. And afterwards on new-builds already designated as

old-builds and about to be dwarfed by bigger blocks right alongside them. Dust. Carcinogenic clouds rinsed by inadequate hoses.

The dust on Fann Street choked plants, coated the prams of infants in filth, and crusted the windows.

'And if it's on our windows,' Emma said, 'it's in our lungs. It's appalling. I live directly opposite. I've had bronchitis and chest pains since the demolition began and there are school children inhaling that dust everyday.'

Asthma attacks keep her up at night. She lives in a state of siege. The assault is unremitting. Dust is a condition of ignorance, the suspension of empathy. It's the weather of the new city, for cyclists in masks, and for an evolutionary species of humanity, now growing gills in preparation for quitting a voluntary euthanasia planet on which the final report will be delivered in the voice of Stephen Hawking.

'Without the support of my neighbours and my son's thirteen-year-old friends, during this last terrible year, I couldn't have coped,' Emma wrote. 'In February 2016, on a school skiing trip to Austria, my son had a massive seizure. We still don't know why but since then he has been terribly unwell, and has suffered hundreds of seizures ... One evening when we had to go to A&E in an ambulance, one of my neighbours did all my washing up so when we returned the next day the kitchen was clean. These things are important when you're going through a traumatic time. One of the elderly neighbours who I got to know in the park offered to drive us to A&E if we ever needed to get there. He had just come out of hospital himself after heart surgery. This is what it means to live in a supportive community.'

'ONE CAN CHOOSE TO LIVE in a place as a sort of visitor,' the poet Gary Snyder said, 'or try to become an inhabitant ... Necessity was the teacher that finally showed us how to live as part of the natural community.' And this happened, painfully, suddenly, as revelation, for Emma: the former migrations, place to place, never satisfactory for more than a couple of years, transmuted into the heroic articulation of a very particular spirit of place. Against adversity. Migration became migraine. And migraine a mandate for resistance.

'The post-war municipal dream of an urban village was a complete success,' Emma said. 'I have neighbours who have lived here since the estate was completed in 1957 and who remember Bowater House being built. The planners talk about the desire to go back to pre-Blitz London.'

What Emma stressed was how residents on the estate, and from neighbouring council blocks too, were supportive of Louis, on a day-to-day basis, as one of their own. The external threat did not bring about her son's absences and seizures, quite the reverse. Under full-frontal assault, the Bowater House community emphasised a determination to cure their problems by their own actions.

'What saddens me is the effect that the Denizen development will have on our estate,' Emma said. 'My experience this last year has shown what it means to live in a community. Louis's friends have been truly amazing. They have shown such empathy and understanding. Thirteen-year-olds, fourteen-year-olds. I don't know how we would have managed without their help. All these boys got to know each other playing in the park after school. Even in winter. It will be very sad to lose the sun at this time.'

The skirmishes rumbled on: appeals, court appearances, points of order, minimal payments in lieu of social housing. Legal process sucks the life out of buildings caught in the battle. The participants weary, sicken, retrench and are fired up once more. Perhaps Shelter will get involved? There will be auctions for the protest banners. Cyclists pause in Fann Street to log the images on their mobile phones. Articles appear in the *Guardian* and the *Mail*. Louis undergoes a PET scan. It takes months to find out what was revealed. Meetings have to be arranged. Consultations. Phones ring unanswered. Emails are spam.

Demolition of Golden Lane Estate.

Early on, as the future loss of light in Fortune Street Park was contemplated, and Bowater House balconies inspired by dreams of Le Corbusier were spun by the developers as unnecessary sunshades, Louis Petit experienced the neuropsychological hallucinations known as Alice in Wonderland syndrome. His hands were visibly growing on the duvet. The ceiling pressed down on the bed. His bedroom stretched like rubber. His arms were not long enough to find his head. It is thought that Lewis Carroll, a perpetual migraine sufferer, exploited similar symptoms for those trippy sections of *Alice's Adventures in Wonderland*. Now it appeared that the city, burrowing compulsively into itself, those giant rabbit chasms of Crossrail, is nothing more than a neuropsychological hallucination of mushrooming overnight towers, absurdist law courts making inequitable judgements, empty green-glass palaces – and a Mad Hatter's Tea Party of fancy-dress diners addressed by goat-faced politicians, schooled in false sincerity, making speeches contrary to everything they know to be true. 'Sentence first – verdict afterwards.' London. Brexit. Golden Lane. Goodbye.

TO DRAW BREATH, step back, make my own PET scan of the City as a pinko-grey mass, pulsing and flickering with conflicting messages, and to evaluate its present health, the success or failure of invasive towers and pits, I walked the old boundary, the tolerated remnants of the Roman wall, west, in the direction of the Barbican – and Golden Lane. If I laid out a map of the compacted topography like a coronal section, scalp as wall, I could navigate the folds and fissures. Long shadows of future developments had more solidity than the hulks to which they were attached. I remembered that remark of James Sallis, quoting Descartes, how all our ills come from 'a man being unable to sit alone, quietly, in a room.' Sitting quietly in a room feels like a special dispensation in contemporary London, where so many rough sleepers are propping up buildings, bedding down to demarcate ATM machines, automatic doors of supermarkets, dripping railway bridges and vaulted hollows under elevated motorways.

Antonio Muñoz Molina captures the way that staying still becomes a pathology: the neurotic walker, struggling to transfer a city's promenades and alleys into a negotiable set of neural pathways, locates the germ of his own mortality.

'The room in shadows was concave and the ceiling low like a cave or basement or the skull that holds his brain, his feverish mind, exhausted from reading and solitary thinking, with all his memories, his physical features, the images of his life, his heart palpitations, the propensity to believe he had contracted a fatal disease, cancer, an angina, the routine of hiding and fleeing.'

In other words, do we walk to take a reading of the health of the buildings, the revised configurations, or to find the right place in which to discard our own sickness? The walk is a negotiation as we try to do justice to what Philip Hoare calls 'the memory of the actuality of the thing'. I carry a camera as an instrument for forgetting, locking the present away. 'For what has been told is finished,' wrote

Anna Seghers in *Transit* (1944), her novel of waiting, of displaced and fugitive exiles in wartime Marseille. 'Only after he's told someone about his journey, will he have crossed that desert once and for all.'

The London walk is my substitute exile. Before the next convulsion. The oases, the tolerated resting places in the City, shaded benches in Finsbury Circus, the hidden springs of the Walbrook, the locked churches, heraldic gates barring access and high walkways running into new barriers: they are all manifestations of the *squeeze*. The City is performing its own autopsy, subverting flow and digging neurotically, while shielding the wounds behind fences decorated with immaculately cultivated boxwood hedges. The eco-terrorism of the garden city – conform, cultivate, belong – has been imposed on the lobes and central sulcus of the City. The hedges, many of which are now available for tricking out the show flat, the dressing of a roof against acid rain and noxious clouds, are *pictures* of hedges: wallpaper hedges, repeat curtains of glistening leaves interrupted by dead-eye lamps and light fittings.

But I can't resist the offer from Randox Health who have taken over an imposing money temple close to Finsbury Circus: DECODE YOUR BODY. DIAGNOSTIC BIOCHIP TECHNOLOGY. SCIENTIFIC INTELLIGENCE FOR YOUR BODY, YOUR LIFESTYLE. I hesitate for a moment. Do I really want to know the worst? Then I consider how this instant quackery is informed by its surroundings. In this case, marble pillars and a set of imposing steps. Money breeds neurosis, breeds money. Fitness clubs, gyms, in-house massage, chiropractors, health professionals as wacky as anything in Ben Jonson, they infest the City. BE THE FRONTRUNNER OF YOUR HEALTH. City survival as an athletic discipline.

The whole business should probably be done online, right up to surgery and death certificate, but I'm old fashioned. I love a substantial catalogue. The priestess, in white, struggles to locate such an anachronistic item. My consultancy period is already over. WELCOME TO THE FUTURE OF WELLBEING. The promise is to identify signs of illness before they manifest, *before* they exist. To anticipate the shadow on the lung before the alien growth is even a bud. Dis-ease is a detectable imbalance: such as my relationship with developments along London Wall. TAKE CONTROL OF YOUR SEXUAL HEALTH IN PRIVATE.

The plaque for Bedlam is still there, pitiful spectres of the falling sickness. And the promise on the fence that blocks my detour: EXPLORE THE BARBICAN. THIS ICONIC LANDMARK AND OASIS IN THE HEART OF THE CITY IS YOURS TO ENJOY. But not now, not today. Expensively rusted bridges span discontinued walkways. C502 LORRY HOLDING AREA.

Cyclists, high on pollutants, gagging on tarry particulates mainlined into the bloodstream, jump the lights. London Wall, once a ditch, is now an abyss. Some of the Chinese visitors are wearing protective masks. They don't help. We are sucking the poison straight from exhaust pipes. Traffic is at a standstill. Over the dedicated cycle lane and across a line of yellow hurdles, I spot the ghostly outline of the Roman wall: a taproot anchored in the clay.

A STEP OR TWO AWAY from the hideous road, and to the side of an underground car park where waiting chauffeurs vape, preferring their own toxins to the emissions on general offer, there is a curved wall of rose-red bricks, a jagged bastion against the free-market glaciation of the blue-ice towers. Trying to navigate a path towards the water features of the Barbican, the marooned church, the permitted walkways, I find myself in the Barbers' Physic Garden. The barber-surgeons of the sixteenth and seventeenth centuries were a City Company dedicated to preserving their own status, privileges and inherited mystique. Butchery and healing were twinned, the saw and the spade. Surgeons were often plantsmen and collectors of curiosities. That this garden among the heritaged ruins can still be visited is a victory of sorts.

Brutal or beautiful? The Barbican Estate was designed by Chamberlin, Powell & Bon, whose young architects also built the nearby Golden Lane Estate for the Corporation of the City of London.

I stoop to read the notices pegged beside individual plants, the prescriptions. *Valeriana officinalis (Valerian)* has 'a sedative action and was formerly used for anxiety states'. Obviously we will need bushels of the stuff, those broad serrated leaves, deeply veined. 'Attractive to rats.' And recommended for migraine and insomnia. Make up pillows of dried out herbs for Bowater House. 'It is thought that the Pied Piper of Hamelin may have kept valerian roots in his pockets.'

Like the rats, I make my way towards water. In the late-afternoon gloom, there is an attractive melancholy to the Barbican's enclosed ponds, reflections of drowned blocks, submerged corners of second-century wall. Medicinal plants in the Physic Garden heal by text not ingestion. We have to stop, get down on our knees, and strain our eyes to make the transcription. To think a cure. *That there is a cure for life*. Plants against buildings. Pacific Yew trees against cancer. Hyssop for the stomach. Foxgloves for irregularities of the heart. Virginian Skullcap as an anti-spasmodic. Against convulsions and seizures.

The botanical specimens in this garden were first catalogued in the illustrated *Herball, or Generall Historie of Plantes* written by John Gerard and published in 1597. Gerard, who kept a garden in Holborn, spoke of 'remedies for deep wounds'. His confidence in the science of the time reminds us that we are still wounded, still walking after improbable cures. The herbalist was first an apprentice barber-surgeon, then a botanist, and finally an author (accused of plagiarism, unacknowledged borrowings from Pietro Andrea Mattioli, L'Obel and others). Gerard contrived fantastic illustrations, such as a barnacle tree bearing geese. Producing a definitive work was a way of securing his legacy: name and legend staked to the ground for all to read.

Despite his boast of acquiring knowledge of plants after extensive travels, assertions supported by his patron, the spymaster William Cecil, Lord Burghley, it seems that Gerard rarely strayed far from his Holborn cottage, between Chancery Lane and Fetter Lane. He was embedded in the City, labouring on Burghley's tenement garden. He surrounded himself with a cabal of like-minded friends and associates: politicians, courtiers, herbalists and Huguenots.

The plagiarist, the canny borrower, inspired me. Like Gerard I had never succeeded in straying far from my few yards of London clay. It was time to experience the fiction of travel, to track the radiant city to its original setting beside the Mediterranean Sea, to Le Corbusier.

Radiant City

'The gangrene of decay and collapse advances quickly in
old cities by the sea.'

Antonio Muñoz Molina

SWIMMING MATTERED TO THE FIGURES who mattered to me,
the ones I needed to visit as part of the journey to make
sense of this relationship between buildings and health:
individual wellbeing, cultivated glow, and a more ambitious
grappling after resolution between settled communities
and the places where fate had left them. In a 1971 lecture
on consciousness and psychopathology, the anthropolo-
gist Gregory Bateson said that 'all that stuff' – swimming,
walking up and down mountains, getting sick and getting
well – interlocked. It's like floating, he suggests, being out
there in otherness, seemingly in control, but choosing to
let go.

Many of the characters I was chasing came in the end
to the dazed margin of the sea. And there was always,
behind that accidental or strategic decision, a powerful
residue from childhood, sentiment for a specific location,
a lovely timeless time. The way that children process incidents, frustrations, intense smells, colours and textures that
their parents have completely forgotten. Or never, in the
flurry of the mundane, even registered. A topography of
promenades, arcades, lidos, campsites and cottages where

loaned out kids were deposited with grandparents or eccentric relatives. The magic of Andrew Kötting's round-Britain
Gallivant is the film's centripetal expulsion from the pebbles
of the East Sussex littoral where Gladys, his Kentish granny,
brought him, along with his siblings – at the moment when
child consciousness acknowledges its contract with gravity,
our earth. The given. *Remember this moment. It will never
be better. Here is where we are. For today. For ever.*

Philip Hoare felt like the ideal person to visit when I
came to consider haunted asylums. I knew that he went
into Southampton Water, close to the site of the demolished Royal Military Hospital at Netley, every morning. It
was his survival routine. The regime that sustained health
and peace of mind. Preparation for the work ahead. Philip
returned to the sea, to his childhood home, from a period in
London, the art and punk community in Hackney.

But the writer I was on my way south to visit, a compet-
itive swimmer in his teenage years, had given up on the sea:
Jonathan Meades knew what was in it. And there might also
have been a consideration of the watery fate of the architect
of the quotable building in Marseille where he was now
settled. The Swiss-born painter and applied artist Charles-
Édouard Jeanneret, self-schooled in Paris and elsewhere,
in the noble profession of touting for commissions, came
through eighteen months of an opportunist war marooned
in Vichy, where there were plenty of adequate hotels packed
with other schemers hoping for patronage from whichever
regime happened to be in power. And he secured, at the age
of sixty, after ten fallow years, the Cité Radieuse project of
his pre-war dreams. Raoul Dautry, newly appointed Minis-
ter of Reconstruction and Urbanism, agreed to fund a '*Unité
d'habitation de grande conforme*' vision in the damaged
Mediterranean port of Marseille. Theory would be tested
on ground secured from boulevard to sea, a sequence of
seventeen related blocks in their own parkland.

Le Corbusier (as Jeanneret became), Corbu (familiarly),

Section sketch by Le Corbusier of l'Unité d'habitation,
showing 'sport at the foot of the houses' and areas
for sunlight and water therapy on the roof.

wide-eyed at the audacity of his own genius, arranged to
be photographed as he presented a maquette of the original multi-coloured block, inspiration for so many British
estates, nurseries and hospitals. And he was himself the
maquette for what Meades said that an architect of a certain
era, with designer-magus status, should look like: round
spectacles, horizontally-striped bow tie, balding dome.

Le Corbusier and Meades were always destined to come
together. They had been sparring for years. Meades called
the Swiss architect 'rigorously inauthentic', which was high
praise. He had a thing for plagiarists, 'genuine' plagiarists,
honest thieves, Borgesian rewriters and literary ecologists
forever recycling their own best bits. He savoured Le Corbusier's wartime politicking as the architect-without-portfolio
'shifted unconvincingly between the ever-mutating factions
of French fascism.' But he also defended Corbu, fifty years
after he drowned. 'He might compromise himself but he
never compromised his art ... He was an architect, thus a
promiscuous tart: it goes with the job.'

By the time Meades arrived with his wife, Colette Forder, at a second-floor apartment in l'Unité d'habitation, it was a magnate for pilgrimage. But not yet posthumous. Neither a cathedral nor a museum. 'The place is for architects and architectural students what Santiago de Compostella is for Catholics,' Meades told me. I don't think he meant a good walk spoiled by superstition and a breathless transfusion of chuntering television nonentities on challenge. 'Sometimes you feel that you're living in Carnac or Stonehenge. I have not actually been prodded yet.'

I was joining the procession. I wanted the experience of that 'magnificent' Le Corbusier roof, a measured progress around the panorama of the city, its mountains, money-stadium and shore at sunset. If his eyesight had been a bit better, Meades said, he might have been a serviceable club cricketer. Instead, he worked his chlorine lengths. He swam, sometimes naked, in chalk streams. And now, after the operations, he clocked up the miles on an exercise bicycle, listening to Schubert, and looking at the view.

Swimming and setting, the prospect of the sea, pro-voked deep memories. *An Encyclopaedia of Myself*, with cover snapshot of child author, on guard against the lens, protecting a caravan, is already an anticipation of the dark-suited adult tour (de force) through the sheds and shacks of the Outer Hebrides for the Meades film, *Isle of Rust*. The title is relatively modest – and accurate. *Encyclopaedia* is a list book, picking at scabs of sentiment, the lost country of rogue uncles (some honorary, some blood-inflicted) and cashiered majors (hanging on to their titles, post-war, when there was nothing else left). One of these uncles, Eric, 'kept a boat moored on the Netley shore.' The malign presence of the Southampton military hospital and asylum, all those windows, those corridors, was a useful backdrop for rec-reation onboard a Royal Navy cast-off. 'Uses of: drinking bottled beer and gin on Sundays, and navigating under the influence.' Eric rarely ventured further than his boat. He took the occasional Spanish holiday, removing his leg and sliding into the water.

THE TRAIN JOURNEY, London to Marseille, with a change in Paris, was a romantic notion. And it seemed, at first, to work pretty well. There is less hassle in the station and it takes twenty minutes to get there, as against the grind out to the airport (with punitive toll for the Heathrow Express). The Eurostar delivery chute at St Pancras International, grafted on to the kitsch statuary and shopping malls and help-yourself piano, reminds us of what will be lost to Brexit foolishness: beyond the choking bureaucracy and financial advantages and disadvantages, and fear of invaders, the opening out of cultural exchanges, language, and simple pleasure in difference, in pushing back the horizon.

From the train window, a view on the ever developing, always stalled development: flats have been inserted within the hoop of gas holders, removed from their original position, retained and now occupied after the fashion of similar developments, years back, in Celtic Tiger Dublin. Graffiti has been erased, leaving suspicious white blotches like the aftermath of misguided cosmetic surgery. This zone is an insert, a Euro-aspirational theft from the mess of London, always decaying, always kicking on, entropy and excess, surveillance and insecurity.

Walter Benjamin wrote a feuilleton about reading on rail journeys. The habit was not about pleasure, he reckoned, but the need to appease the gods of the train. The whole enterprise, from departure to destination, is filled with such dread. The traveller is stateless, carrying the wrong papers, forged documents. He (or she) devours the miles too fast and is always late, connections are missed in the 'unpredictable flight of spatio-temporal thresholds.' The arrangement of the carriage emphasises loneliness. Purchasing a book from a station trolley, preferably a yellow splash of detective fiction, will help to overcome anxiety. Benjamin recommends A. K. (Anna Katherine) Green rather than Graham Greene, who wrote *about* trains and gave filmed interviews in them. 'Her short stories are just the same length as the Gotthard Tunnel.'

Chris Petit, who was fond of German trains, always associated the business of travel with the books chosen to accompany the journey (no snap purchases at the station). Berlin to Marseille was defined as the right distance for reacquainting himself with Alfred Döblin's epic *Berlin Alexanderplatz* (a novel named after a station).

I preferred not to read anything beyond the unravelling documentary of landscape, the peripheral tower estates of Paris and the unedited surge of graffiti as we approach Gare du Nord. And then, change made, patterns of shaved fields, low sheds, choppy water in irrigation ditches and ponds: Eurostar halts amputated from the towns they service but attended by ranks of waiting taxis. Paddocks of car parks behind mesh fences. Concrete water towers. All of it under an unrelenting varnish of cement motes, a steady sirocco of industrial scale crop-dusting, the blowback from recent demolitions, contrails of trucks in and out of stone quarries.

I picked at my bilingual guide to *Le Corbusier: L'Unité d'habitation de Marseille*. 'In order to resolve the problem, the French State set up the Ministry of Reconstruction and Urban Planning (MRU) in 1945, headed by Raoul Dautry. The Ministry's objective was to put in place a clearly defined policy aimed at providing a housing solution while modernising France's towns and cities in a way that respected both traditional and avant-garde lines of thinking. Another key goal for MRU was to promote the development of the building industry.' In other words, more plain-suited 'constructeurs' and fewer showboating 'architectes' in bow ties and round glasses.

My companion, Anna Sinclair, was reading a book called *The Vanishing Futurist*, with growing enthusiasm, and breaking off at chapter's end to check the advance in the window. Identifying, at a distance, the anvil shape of Cézanne's Mont Sainte-Victoire and the brand name PAUL plastered over outlets offering patisseries on the station platform, I began to anticipate our twilight arrival in Marseille. Cezanné frequently orientated his compositions by locating the railway bridge from the Aix-Marseille line in the foreground of his paintings. In a letter to his childhood friend Émile Zola in October 1877, he called the view of the mountain from the train a 'beau motif'.

With the first sight of docks and warehouses, I appreciated the old conceit that Marseille was the 'city where Europe ends'. In the mythologised version, a labyrinth of narrow streets and passages, hills and steps, cafés and cheap hotels, displaced persons wait in limbo for their exit visas. They walk. And walk. And wait.

Walter Benjamin, escaping Paris, was one of these; putting on time, carrying his briefcase of papers, before attempting the terrible tramp over the Pyrenees into Spain. Then being turned back and refusing to retreat: an overdose of morphine (the right dose for the job). His friend Anna Seghers, arrested by the Gestapo as a Communist, migrated to Paris and on to Marseille when the Germans invaded northern France. Her novel *Transit*, written in Mexico, after she managed to secure an exit visa, felt timeless. It was not published in Germany until 1948, three years after the author's return to her homeland, to East Berlin. *Transit* was one of the best descriptions of purgatory as a specific geographical setting, a port nobody is ever going to leave for the better place.

Heinrich Böll understood the historic significance of documentation, the transit visa granting the holder permission to *pass through*, but not to remain. As Seghers writes, 'I needed proof of my intended departure so that they would let me stay.' Under these paradoxical conditions, spending hours waiting and walking between borrowed rooms and offices, following ghosts, checking faces through the steamed-up windows of zinc bars, the sickness is inevitable. Marseille incubates the virus of impermanence; doctors are wizards, wise men or fakes, but they have no cures. The characters of the novel are 'forever running from one death toward another'. This is the old city of sailors and immigrants, it does not belong to any country. Doctors, sought out like embassy officials, stampers of forms, have the only passports that mean anything: terminal diagnoses.

'I thought, maybe he really is a good person. And probably just because he is a doctor he believes in healing. But I don't. I don't believe in healing. At least not by this doctor … In my mind I turned to the dead man: We'll take her away from him soon. Rest assured, he won't keep her long.'

Joseph Conrad knew the lethargy of Marseille, the best location in which to experiment with recklessness and despair, gestures of petty criminality rehearsing future fictions. Above the Vieux Port, the displaced Pole sleepwalked between the stages of an unresolved life. Maya Jasanoff, in the *Dawn Watch: Joseph Conrad in a Global World*, describes the moment in the putative writer's career when he is hoping for employment, a berth, squandering his allowance and composing letters to beg for further funds.

'Konrad walked down the hill from his lodgings to the Vieux Port. Masts poked above the roofline like shorn wheat. He walked past cafés of clacking dominoes and twinkling glasses of vermouth, peasant women holding panniers of goat cheese for sale, an old North African cranking his barrel organ over the dissonant screech of trams. In and out of shipping offices came the captains, faces creased like old papers. Knuckles of sun punched the water in the harbor.'

Conrad had the wrong papers for a French vessel. Inspectors rejected them and he was put ashore. He threw the last of his cash into a foolhardy investment, running contraband to Spain. Everything was lost. He came to London.

'He would never write the truth of what happened in Marseille,' Jasanoff said. Reading her account of these days, the picaresque travelling shot down the hill, I am conscious of the biographer's own footfall. A woman, with a book to deliver, making careful notes and following ghosts.

COMING OUT OF GARE SAINT-CHARLES with our bags, we struck off in the general direction of the Vieux Port. I noted the grand entry steps we hadn't used, additions that contradicted the workaday aspects of the station. They belonged in the Netflix version of *Marseille*, the boxed set in which an impressively gargantuan Gérard Depardieu is wheeled around like an Empire period armoire in clever tailoring, in order to ballast a series of spectacular backdrops: harbour, gilded Madonna of Notre-Dame de la Garde, Velodrome. Backdrops against which politicians in dark glasses, fixers and criminals from the ethnic underclass, plot and scheme and smoke.

There was a satisfactory edge to the streets, to the magic hour when, at home in Hackney, bandits on bicycles emerge, scooter raiders circle, and knife attack horrors occur outside betting shops, under railway bridges. We followed a good father, hand in hand with his young son, setting out, perhaps, for cinema or restaurant. The boy had a trusting dignity to his stride. He didn't bounce or tug or make demands. The father unrolled the rubber mat he carried under his arm, and arranged the optimum position for his son, and the saucer for the evening's begging, as the promenaders took to the streets. He brushed the rubber, with deliberation, before he settled the unmoving boy for his long stint. Armed police were gathering also, checking their equipment, chatting, stamping their feet, uninterested in whatever was happening here.

We found ourselves on Canebière, heading in the direction we wanted, towards the lights of the Vieux Port. A substantial and familiar thoroughfare, with the shops found everywhere, banks, tourist office, foot traffic, and doorways punctuated by subdued and uninsistent beggars, professionals staying within the space allotted to them.

The drums got louder as we approached the waterfront. Now, from behind, we were caught in a tidal surge of marchers with banners demanding freedom for the moustached Kurdish nationalist leader, Abdullah Öcalan. The chanting faded as the procession swerved to the left along the harbour. A convoy of waiting police vans parked behind obstacles set up to deter rogue vehicles from driving at the crowd. These drummers and flag-wavers were following Kurdish marches in other European cities, protesting the Turkish offensive in Syria.

After dumping our bags, we set off to find a street I noticed on the fold-out Marseille guide donated by our hotel receptionist: Cours J. Ballard. One method I used for rapid orientation in an unknown or inadequately known city – Seattle, Paris – was to walk from the centre to the nearest Ballard (or Balard in Paris), somewhere on the periphery (where the future reveals itself), as a nod to the late Shepperton author. It usually paid off. But the splendid Marseille nameplate was not a tribute to JG, in acknowledgement of *Super-Cannes* and holidays spent at Antibes, reading, resting, eating out and driving around hilltop villages where great artists lived. As well as making sharp-eyed research trips to marinas, apartment complexes and the Pierre Cardin Foundation at Miramar, described by Ballard as 'one of the strangest buildings in Europe'. There was an abiding fascination with the 'whole terrain of science parks and autoroutes on the high ground above the Var plain.' Those holidays were never wasted. Ballard loved the faded glitz, the corrupted terrain, the 'mineral light and vivid air'. The Riviera, Ballard said, 'was one of the last places where people could behave badly.'

Names migrate and resettle. The narrator of *Super-Cannes* is called Dr Sinclair. But the Ballard honoured here, on the south side of Vieux Port, was the poet, Jean, founder and editor of *Les Cahiers du Sud*, an influential magazine offering publication to assorted surrealists and others washed up in the early days of the war: André Breton, René Crevel, Paul Éluard, Benjamin Péret, Antonin Artuaud, Henri Michaux. The editor's boasted creed was: 'our will to refute'.

After the fire that greeted his arrival at l'Unité d'habitation, an all too literal house-warming, Jonathan Meades moved, with Colette Forder, and whatever he was allowed to retrieve from his second-floor apartment, to a spacious flat close to Cours Jean Ballard. Sensible insurance set them up in a lively and central environment for six months, before they were allowed to return to Cité Radieuse. The fire, in February 2012, was started by papers placed too close to a heater – the winter months are chilling – in a first-floor duplex. Fire services fought the blaze for twelve hours. Eight residential units were gutted, several others seriously smoke damaged. There was no loss of life, five residents were treated in hospital. Thanks to high-specification materials and good design, the building survived and made a complete recovery. There was no Grenfell Tower crematorium chimney tragedy.

Many meals enjoyed in the area we were exploring, and elsewhere along the coast, gave weight to Jonathan's hint that bouillabaisse should be avoided at all costs, in favour of the much older local speciality, pizza. But having recently indulged in a rich, sopping, multi-tentacled stew in Hastings, I wanted to make the comparison. Meades was right. The atmosphere in the harbourside bistro was authentic – piracy with mild derision – and the wine flowed. It had been a long day. I imagined a few hours of winter sunshine, escape from invading weather systems from the east, for tomorrow's expedition to Le Corbusier's admired experiment in communal living, the point of our journey, but Anna was better informed. She said that it would rain, early and often.

I dropped at once into a deep sleep and was visited in a dream by J. G. Ballard. He looked good, fit and easy moving. His hair was shorter and trimmer than in life. He wore loose white trousers and a white shirt, open at the neck. He might have been a cosmetic surgeon from California or the spokesperson for a new religion. He said that he was presently 'in decent digs' near a cemetery in Paris. From the way he described the business of the district, I thought of Ménilmontant and Père Lachaise. Ballard also said that he had surprised himself by missing Shepherd's Bush, the honest grot of Goldhawk Road. He quite fancied a Chinese. As ever, he refused to give out any details of the current work in progress, but clearly it was going well. He thought quite often of his favourite beaches. And was almost resolved to take up swimming as a regular discipline. Or absolution. He said that he wouldn't bother me again.

ANNA WAS ON THE MONEY. We stepped out next morning into a light, persistent drizzle. With her years of experience in Hackney schools, my wife was interested in the orderly crocodile of hand-holding children being shepherded through the weather down the side of Vieux Port towards some improving cultural manifestation. The ferry across the harbour was inoperative, a minor technical problem, they explained. But the tuk-tuk-tuk sound was locked in my head, bringing back the way Jean-Luc Godard dealt with Marseille and Vieux Port in about one minute at the opening of *A Bout de Souffle*. The crash barriers were not then in place. There were no look-at-me intrusions, like that polished steel pavilion, inverting the passing throng, conjured by Norman Foster as part of the collateral damage attendant on being European City of Culture. Late 1950s and Marseille, in Raoul Coutard's black-and-white photography (pushed 35mm still stock) was a working port. Belmondo reads a newspaper, smokes, strokes his lip, hotwires an American car, and away. The open road. The lines of poplars. Motorbike policeman shot and killed. Marseille, with its drift population of Corsicans, North Africans, embedded Italians, is a suburb of Paris, of Pigalle. But on the soundtrack, for just a moment, you catch the tuk-tuk-tuk chug of the ferry and the humped outline of the fort at the harbour mouth – towards which, drenched by a near biblical downpour, we were now heading. Godard's genius was to tap the real and move on: tear-it-up tabloid cinema. As poetry. As quotation. As performance. Marseille is done in less time than it takes to type this sentence. We were in town for one day. But it would take a lifetime of wandering and hanging around to represent the port adequately in a paragraph. The more you know, the fewer words you have to use.

Rain matured into snow. The sensation of being slowly saturated under a cold shower was localised, melting flakes dribbling down the neck, ice droplets from the sodden blotter of my cap. The Madonna perched on her high tower, a circus seal on a golden ball, up on that plug of rock, the limestone outcrop, was caught for an instant between buildings and traffic and then gone. Clutching her infant, she loomed over the port, a potential jumper trembling on the brink of taking a step into space. It had been at the back of my mind, if all went smoothly, to make the pilgrims' climb to Notre-Dame de la Garde, and to experience the sweep of the port and the town, to orientate ourselves in the direction of the Radiant City. To prepare for the afternoon's tour and the dinner with Jonathan Meades.

Defeated by the conditions, the blizzard was getting personal, and stocked up from an excellent Casino supermarket, we were about to retreat to our hotel, when I noticed steps advertising some sanctioned route to the Romanesque-Byzantine basilica. Visibility was down to a couple of yards. We gripped the clammy handrail and hauled ourselves up the slippery ascent. It was like becoming part of the snaking procession on the approved postcard: cowled monks, dignitaries and drummers, bearing the Madonna aloft on her way to the uncompleted church.

Sharp crystals crusted our shoulders. Trees and bushes drooped with the sudden weight of snow. There was no view beyond the path: we were ticking off the stations of the cross in the ideal penitential conditions. Agonised statuary felt frostbite on naked limbs. The Jesus on the plinth raised his finger to the sky in disbelief. Stepped access to the basilica was forbidden by incident tape and a raised drawbridge. The few tourists – mainly Chinese – who made it up here had nothing to photograph. Even selfies didn't register in the apocalyptic whiteout.

The Marseille snowfall, the first in years, helped to enforce the rule of silence. The interior of the church on the rock, designed by Henri Espérandieu and completed by his student Henri Révoli, was a fabulous collision of stripes and stars, anchors and mosaic inlays, arches, curves and golden domes, reminiscent of a re-dedicated Turkish bathhouse. Visitors moved slowly and with care, reminded at every step that Notre-Dame de la Garde oversaw the Vieux Port and the fishing boats.

In the upper church, after we had emerged from the dimly lit crypt, we were greeted by Neo-Byzantine abstractions, columns, pilasters. Supplicants, older women in black, were muttering their prayers beside a wall of ex-voto paintings. Having tested ourselves with the steep climb, we were rewarded by an exhibition of tightly packed representations, categorised into sea, air, land, as records of miraculous cures, successful intercessions by the Madonna of the bell tower. There were no crutches, prosthetic limbs or bandages on display. Instead we found portraits of vessels, dioramas and letters of evidence.

The church walls host a pictorial history of the port and its inhabitants. Deepwater cod fishermen, surviving an Atlantic storm, know that they must climb to the church, sometimes barefoot, with an accurate model of their ship.

Notre-Dame de la Garde.

The ex-voto offerings are a negotiation with fate, hung in uneven lines, in their gilded frames. The Good Mother intervenes, at sickbeds, down shadowy streets, in the small hours of the night. She flares through the darkness of the oil paint like a dying light bulb. The nave is hung with modelled ships, yachts, three-masters, tiny aircraft spinning on strings, floating as if in a drowned cathedral.

The upper terrace was closed as a hazard in this weather, but when we emerged into the open air, the snow had stopped, the white mist had blown away, and the city was revealed. Identifying the aerodynamic whaleback of the Velodrome on Boulevard Michelet, we plotted the route we would take to find the Cité Radieuse.

THE LE CORBUSIER BLOCK was a different, more secular pilgrimage. The devoted came with their cameras and notebooks, but there was no rock to climb, no steps to manage; nobody draped the mesh fence around the tennis

Unité d'habitation, Marseille.

court with ex-voto offerings, paintings of burnt apartments, plumes of smoke, five-hour operations survived.
Boulevard Michelet was well served by buses and trams.
Cité Radieuse was not the shining city on the hill, but
an ordinary human hive, self-sufficient and functional,
a model for so many others. Without this attention to
detail, the considered specifications, the space and the
light, the lesser versions crashed, atrophied into ruin, sur-
vivalism and sickness. The rectangular box with the 337
units, habitat for around 1,200 people, living, working,
moving through the foyer, the lifts, the interior street of
shops and social facilities, has achieved, since its construction (1945–52), the status of a canonised natural
feature. I was conscious too that this building was
never social housing. It was occupied, from the start,
by teachers, civil servants, architects and professionals:
those who understood the initial pitch and had an interest in sustaining the myth of the good place. Like an
exhibit brought to life, a set of theoretical propositions
tested and proved, l'Unité d'habitation was an inspiration for public housing, but was never made available to
the spectrum of the Marseille public for which, in a period
of recovery and retrenchment, it might have been intended.
There is a hotel, a restaurant (not favoured by Meades), a
bookshop promoting all things Le Corbusier, and several
designer outlets. L'Unité feels more like a secure and crafted
village enterprise than a city within the city.

In a letter to Albert Camus, written in 1957, the architect
said: 'I'm taken with the idea of a "Box of miracles" … It is a
rectangular box made of concrete. It doesn't have any of the
traditional theatrical tricks, but the possibility, as its name
suggests, to make miracles.' The Cité Radieuse, as conceived,
was related to Le Corbusier's early experiences, clutching his
Ruskin, at the Carthusian monastery outside Florence.

Now the sky was cloudless, the approved intensity of
Mediterrean blue required to show off the whiteness of the

block and its grid of repeated primary colours. L'Unité was reminiscent of Bowater House and the Golden Lane Estate, but with adequate breathing space and poplars, with scale and spectacle unthreatened by spectres of mindless infill and London's uncontrolled mishmash of riverside towers (even in districts without a view of the Thames). It was hard to believe that this amble around the Cité Radieuse was still the day of snowfall and that slithering, grasping climb to Notre-Dame de la Garde. On the edge of the north–south boulevard, chopped and leafless plane trees were sculpted to set off l'Unité and its neighbour, Le Brasilia, a private commission, sympathetic to Corbu; its curves inspired by the architect Fernand Boukobza's visit to the Brazilian capital. Roughcast concrete spiral staircases are both signature design elements and practical fire escapes.

'Stare at anything long enough and it becomes fantastical,' Meades said, quoting Flaubert (with a nod to Andy Warhol). Stare *out* from one of the balconies of l'Unité, posed against your colour-coded *brise-soleil*, and you become enmeshed in the view. It's addictive and counter-motivational. Why stir? Everything you need has been provided. When, as the evening became cooler, Colette moved across to pull down the insulated silver-foil (Warholist) blind, to retain the day's warmth a little longer, while killing the vision framed in the window, Anna begged for a reprieve. 'Can we leave it as it is?' We were in no hurry to rise from the table.

ON ARRIVAL AT CITÉ RADIEUSE, we circled the block, respectfully, at a certain distance: the park, the plantings, the empty tennis courts behind the mesh fence. We sat on a bench. I liked the way the building floated, elevated by its piloti, carrying the gaze upward. Bands of sunlight striped a patchwork floor: the concrete nave, supporting the entire structure, was open on all sides. In Hackney, the Xeroxed versions of this design, fudging tight budgets, packed the equivalent space with utilities and bins, pulling estate blocks down into the gravity of London.

Units of scale were based on Le Corbusier's Modular proportions; a thesis given physical form by a red-and blue-dolmen against which random walkers photographed so well – as did the architect's hieratic figures, his Picasso 'tributes' pressed into concrete panels like fossils of a future broad-shouldered pinhead race. 'In nature, every organism's dimensions are proportioned in relation to its surroundings,' Corbu said.

WE PASSED UNCHALLENGED into the foyer. The lifts were capacious and they worked. Our fellow passengers, young women, were polite. The long, low-lit corridor, rubbery and soft underfoot, was unthreatening. Green iceboxes, chest-high outside every flat, punctuated the dim tunnel. They were designed to keep the building cool in the early days. Two girls, skating and chatting, gave us a courteous salute. I identified the source of the oddity: the corridor was the lower deck of an ocean liner. The apartments were cabins.

Jonathan offered the tour. He was dressed in black, something loose, round-necked and easy fitting: rehearsal mode. Very much like an actor, or ballet master in down-time, between energy-sapping performances for the camera. And the outfits necessary to his brand and practised delivery: clipped, audible, provocative. Intelligent. He did not like the term 'presenter'. This is not what he did: neither a 'wow, awesome' oxygen-waster rendered inarticulate by lambs and waterfalls, nor an arm-waving stand-in-the-way of the art, spout-the-bleeding-obvious nuisance with hat and scarf. Meades stayed in character. He had an argument to make. He tailored his scripts to what he could get away with. And then, of course, a little more. The black garb was for exercise bike, laptop labours, attending to dangerous cacti on the loggia.

We appreciated the time he was giving us after a recent procedure for implanting a stent in an artery. This took about an hour in a good Marseille hospital. The surgeon guides a thin wire through a catheter to the treatment site, the area of blockage, and inflates a tiny balloon. When the doctor is satisfied, balloon catheter, guide wire and guide catheter will be removed. When we made our visit, Jonathan was recovering from a seasonal cold.

The couple lived in one of the largest apartments, originally intended for – but never occupied by – a three-generational family. There was space to move about, to make paintings and transfer them to the computer for revision. A good way to clear blockages, hit the flow, before pushing on with the novel or the next script on the architecture of Franco. I liked the title of the show of large pieces Meades exhibited in Redchurch Street, Shoreditch: *Ape Forgets Medication.* 'When a work is begun there is seldom any conception of where it will lead ... It is the very opposite of how he writes – fretfully, costively, and with a willingness to starve to death of syphilis in a garret for the sake of an adverb.' (The man provides his own copy.)

We sat down to an excellent dinner: quality lamb, 'Elephant Gratin' (one of the dishes from *The Plagiarist in the Kitchen*), white cakes of the goat cheese Rocamadour, followed by strawberries and tartlets. There is a weekly market on the boulevard and good shops to hand. If Jonathan needs to walk, he takes the car. A true Ballardian.

After many years in London, Meades wearied of it, what the sprawl had become. There was a certain inevitability about his occupation of a flat in this building. The apartment swam with light. Jonathan and Colette were hospitable. The conversation at the table included summoned presences no longer with us: Jonathan's close friend Snoo Wilson (whose heart gave out when he was running for a train at Ashford), Robin Cook (aka Derek Raymond) shaping his return to the underside of London, or a dream of it, while labouring in a French vineyard. And the bookman/bluesman Martin Stone, mesmerising the company with erudite gossip when he visited with another old chum, Nigel Burwood, who was unreliably rumoured to have employed Meades as bookshop manager in his first Hammersmith shop.

It felt as if all the characters I tried to write about had preceded me; they came to Marseille or planned to come here, to eat and talk and acknowledge the magic. The Petits stayed a while. Chris and Louis played tennis down there on that deserted court, by the hour. I wondered if anybody had struck a ball since that time. It was like the end of *BlowUp*: sound as memory. Emma was photographed, hair blowing, on the roof at sunset.

In *Tender Buttons* (1914), Gertrude Stein crafted eccentric word-portraits of culinary terms. 'Dining is west,' she wrote. 'It was a shame it was a shame to stare to stare ...' We sat, comfortably, perhaps too long (too long), and we did stare stare: west. Towards Parc Borely, the plage and the sea. It was time to catch the golden hour on the roof. I imagined a frisson of relief when we said that we could find the way for ourselves. Jonathan had cooked and guided us through the spaces of the flat, but his energies, after the operation and the winter cold, were finite. He did not need to see what was up there, or out there, and it was tactful to leave us to it.

The architect and the planners had laid out, with scrupulous attention to detail, this machine for living. For good health. Carrying solid insurance and with faith in French medicine, Meades arrived here and almost immediately came down with pleurisy, which evolved into a pulmonary embolism and the drama of a five-hour operation. The sort of serious undertaking from which the patient emerges as a new or revised personality. I wouldn't try to explain it, but I recognise the fact that after a period of concentrated work (when no ills or failures of nerve are permitted), and when the break finally comes, the rest, holiday, clearing of the desk, our physical systems crash. The sickness that has been hovering in the wings strikes with a vengeance.

'THE ROOF OF L'UNITÉ is a transcendent work,' Meades wrote in *Museum Without Walls*: 'It is as though Odysseus is beside you. In a few gestures it summons the entirety of the Mediterranean's mythic history ... It is exhilarating and humbling, it occasions aesthetic bliss. It demonstrates the beatific power of great art, great architecture.'

And this is true. Meades' eyesight might not have been sharp enough for cricket, but it is quite capable of recognising the Homeric when he sees it. A turn around this deck, where ventilation shafts are concrete sculptures meant to invoke the cruise-liner lifestyle ... sauntering before dinner, no medication forgotten, exercising before breakfast, play zones for kiddies, city spread out like the arrival of the dream of the good life ... confirms the proposition: a well conceived, well executed building *in the right place* will freeze time. Suspend disbelief. A temporary remission from mortality, the life sentence. Measure your length of stride.

Like Godard in *Le Mépris (Contempt)*, when he has Fritz Lang process the terrace above the wine-dark sea, Meades is seduced by setting. In Godard's film – a story borrowed from Moravia, tricked out to justify his location, the Casa Malaparte in Capri – disparate characters are trying to put together a version of *The Odyssey*. There is no other story, voyage and return.

For some reason nobody can explain, Casa Malaparte was the working model for the only significant structure on the prize-winningly nude Hastings pier, the one after the fire. The stepped Capri villa with the flat roof where Bardot sunbathed became a coffee stall, tourist-and-heritage shop and exhibition space in East Sussex. It commanded a splendid view of the other great boat-building, Marine Court, as the dying sun obliged over Eastbourne.

Built between 1936 and 1938 from designs by Kenneth Dalgleish and Roger K. Pullen, architects nobody outside the business has ever bothered about, Marine Court was the ultimate Art Deco cruise liner in concrete, a landlocked avatar of the Cunard White Star *Queen Mary*. The borough engineer Sidney Little, known as 'The Concrete King', has accrued most of the posthumous credit for visionary vandalism: tearing down major chunks of Burton St Leonards to impose an anchored iceberg, the tallest block of residential flats in Britain. Light was stolen, as ever, from innocent terraces on the slopes behind this magnificently ill-conceived invader.

Marine Court anticipated Corbusier's Radiant City. And the current cruise-liner invasion of Europe's ports from Palermo to Barcelona – and soon London. But instead of keeping the promenade deck clear and open to achieve the transcendence Meades commends, the roof of Marine Court was barnacled with radio masts, photovoltaic scanners, humming disks and carcinogenic boosts in every anti-aesthetic shape and size. You could feel the bread self-toasting five floors down. The building was alive: with ghosts. Faces appeared from nowhere in the weird portholes of maze-like corridors. Lifts worked on their own. And stalled between floors when humans rode them.

Sidney Little believed that concrete and good health were linked: the seafront, Hastings to Bulverhythe, was a curated underpass exploiting the brief interlude before swimming, naked hiking and sleeping under the stars turned sinister. And Little's 'Bottle Alley', decorated by the town's unemployed and vagrant population with bottles they had previously emptied or found, morphed into a monstrous defensive-aggressive seawall on the other side of the Channel. Those round bastions looking out on Hastings pier referenced bunker forts, submarine pens and machine-gun nests. *Béton brut*. Marine Court was launched in the right harbour at the wrong time. In the war years its flats were occupied by the military, the cruise ship was commandeered like one of those troop vessels sent to the Falklands.

The original pitch was shipboard romance for metropolitan weekenders. Port out, starboard home: first-class cabins were sea-facing, servants were in hutches at the rear under the cliff. Tunnels beneath the road deposited fortunate voyagers in sun lounges on the shingle, with no requirement to confront locals or day-trippers. Even with the post-war concrete cancers, discriminations of rust, failing boilers, clapped-out lifts, something of the original fantasy survived. In bed, you were out at sea. Washing the dishes, you drifted over a Cubist jigsaw of roofs and windows. But health ... the convalescence of the ocean ... swimmers and leisurely promenaders working up a thirst for cocktails ...

On my first day sleeping in a flat in Marine Court, I met a poet I knew in Dublin, forty years before, back from the dead. He had been through good times as playwright, filmmaker, producer: now he was lodged at the top of the building, with uncompleted scripts, books the last local dealers wouldn't take and a big screen (borrowed from a pub) for watching streamed rugby from everywhere. My friend had been a player and was still fit. He jogged to Bexhill and back, complaining about the ugliness of the shore-protecting interventions along the way.

One morning when I ran into him, placing his football bets in the mini-mart, as I came back from an early swim, he told me that he was not so well. Within weeks, he was dead. The building seemed to be occupied by spectres from discontinued scripts, decent exiles looking bemused on the wrong floor, waiting for a lift that isn't going to come. One night a half-naked man, punctured by needles and tubes, wandered off the balcony into the filmmaker's flat. Wrong medication. Confusion. Then a ninety-three-year-old man, Sven-Olof Legnelius, went over the balcony from his sixth-floor apartment. He lay out there for eight hours in a pool of blood. A younger man was arrested on suspicion of murder.

'WE ARE CONTROLLED by buildings,' Meades said. 'The majority of them are curtailments. They are monolithic. Provisional gaols ... Places are, on the other hand, heterogeneous and multipartite ... Places are feasts for the spirit.'

But the roof walk around l'Unité at sunset is pure architecture: building and place in compliant dialogue. Green rays are out at the edge of things. A generous allocation of space in which nothing cluttered happens. Ocean-liner metaphors hark back to pre-war days when such shameless luxury was possible, before vessels down in the port and along the docks were the best hope of escape; carrying Anna Seghers, for example, to Mexico. Where her book could be completed.

And it was in that Homeric tremor, as an old man in August 1965, that Le Corbusier drowned. His body was washed up on the beach at Roquebrune-Cap Martin, below the modernist villa designed by the Irish architect Eileen Gray and her lover, Jean Badovici. The visionary of the Radiant City had suffered a heart attack, so it appeared, fifty yards from shore. The backstory could sit alongside all the Greek myths of place: thwarted love, jealousy, obsession, revenge. While Gray was absent, Corbu defaced her property with crude phallocentric murals. He painted naked, a jagged cicatrice from an accident with a yacht's propellor gleamed on his right thigh. (He arranged to have the disconcerting portrait taken: nudist in architect's round spectacles.) Bored German troops, occupying the property, shot up the daubs. One of the more blatantly offensive efforts was restored by Jean Broniarski in 1978, in order to emphasise the swastika thought to be latent in the original.

The great architect of l'Unité d'habitation, the boat-building that sails on through spaces where the other blocks of the Cité Radieuse were never built, was inspired early by the silence of monastic life. He built himself a hermit's cabin, close to E-1027, the Eileen Gray house, so that he could wait and watch. Strike out and swim.

OUT

Southampton Water

'And in the effort of praying I have felt as though something in me
had broken, to give me the power of healing ... '

Haniel Long

HE IS IN HIS MOTHER'S HOUSE. But Philip Hoare knows just
how he got there, back to Southampton, a respectable,
status secure suburb, well away from the fading glamour
of Beck Road in pre-hipster Hackney. Well in advance of
the beards, the barista shamen, vegan pubs and discrimi-
nating archaeologists of vinyl. The compulsive Tourette's
tweeterati reporting on every breath taken, hot to miscom-
municate, shame or boost.

Philip knew that he belonged at the water's edge, swimming the busy channel, the bilge discharges and warm
currents from the oil refinery, and looking back, making
reluctant landfall at the place where the vaunting military
hospital of Netley, wings spread like the Angel of the South,
once stood.

This man was at home among the ghosts. He stalked
the vanished but psychically imprinted corridors of the
public park. He scavenged tangled woodland, unrecorded
burial mounds, the midden of the notorious D Wing
lunatic asylum, for trophies to carry back, on his bicycle,
to his mother's house in Sholing. He kept his distance from
mobile phones and tablets. When I came to Southampton

Central station, Philip advised me that he would be waiting on the 'seaward side', where no sea was visible. There might be a vinegar residue on the breeze.

Another train. This time alone. And this time there was a book, a book by Philip Hoare: *Spike Island: The Memory of a Military Hospital*. The definitive account of Netley, a demolished monster whose shadow had haunted me since I read the story in which Sherlock Holmes made his first appearance. The narrator, Doctor Watson, introduces himself. 'In the year 1878 I took my degree of Doctor of Medicine of the University of London, and proceeded to Netley to go through the course prescribed for surgeons in the army.' After being seriously wounded in the Afghan war, Watson's status changes to invalid, to convalescent, putting on time, a London watcher like Poe's 'Man of the Crowd' – before accepting his curse as author and general practitioner.

WE MET MIDWAY across the Atlantic, not swimming but flying down to Mexico, to a literary festival in Guadalajara. The unearned space was a challenge. I recognised my fellow traveller from the author photographs on his books. And from characteristic knee-length shorts and SAVE THE WHALE T-shirt. We fell into conversation between rounds of drinks and plastic trays of unnecessarily enticing food samples, silvery surprises securely packaged as for a Space Shuttle. What impressed me was Philip's revelation that he had managed a swim in Southampton Water *that* morning, before getting to Heathrow for a 9.30 a.m. flight. A night swim, under the stars, to confirm his regime, the jolt to the senses endured at all seasons, in all weathers. The hazard required for a properly balanced life.

I appreciated that Philip Hoare was a younger man by fifteen years, but his method of staying fit and alert felt familiar. The process seemed to be about making the first move of the day at first light – or, in Philip's case, much earlier than that: naked immersion in Southampton Water in the small hours, when the double tide was at its highest point. And the chimney of the oil refinery on the far shore still flared. This wool-capped man of the city, after parking his bicycle, stripped off and struck out, according to conditions and mood, towards a particular channel marker.

My own early circuits of Hackney did not translate very comfortably to the hotel where the writers were settled in Guadalajara. When we met on the station platform in Southampton, Philip told me that he performed his naked swim in the Mexican hotel's too blue pool in the middle of the night. I admired his bravery, when I passed him, wearing trunks now, doing gentle breaststroke laps right alongside the spread tables where Irvine Welsh, Philippa Gregory and British Council facilitators were taking their leisurely breakfasts, chatting and complaining, before cabbing off for another day of interviews and readings at the conference centre. Welsh's sessions turned into riots of tribal enthusiasm, the hall so rammed that excluded autograph fiends rushed the stage, beating aside any obstacles between themselves and the charismatic author.

I tried a walk, but it didn't work. I kept thinking about the Belgian artist Francis Alÿs in Mexico City, rattling along with a revolver in his hand, waiting to be stopped or assaulted, and then refilming the episode as a twin-screen production. Or how he set up a circle of sheep to parade around a public square. Or pushed a block of ice until it disappeared. I accepted an invitation, made by a newspaper, to do my own hike, edge to edge, across Mexico City – but, after they had looked into the security required, the offer was quietly withdrawn.

I had no idea how to infiltrate my Hackney circuit into this fragrant city with its unlearned codes. It worked in continental Europe and down the Pacific coast, from Vancouver to Los Angeles, but not here. Around the hotel there were bursts of scarlet poinsettias, heady clumps of Aztec marigolds and shaded avenues with peeling offers of tarot readings on lighting poles. The latest and glossiest Mercedes-Benz 4WD was parked at a 45-degree angle across the pristine marble steps of a cash-washing dealership. There were very few people. Night workers going home.

I couldn't get a purchase on this place. Transported in serviced luxury, I had never really arrived. Tall buildings swayed with imported entitlement: vanity blocks of narco-architecture in multinational bling, borrowed Las Vegas hotels burnished in gold and the dark-windowed offices of regional government. Further out, towards the airport and beyond, there were sprawling vegetable stands, sheds piled with fruit, Inca Cola franchises and car repair operations. None of this made sense when set against something much older and fiercer and still to be defined.

Brought up in the Catholic faith, Philip must have been amused to find himself swimming beside a disnatured lawn, fountain-sprayed, clipped to perfection, and occupied by a life-sized troop of holy-family figures cast in grey stone. A Mesoamerican Madonna, hands clasped in prayer. A Shoreditch Jesus guy hanging out with a crew of beat angels. And a barbecue shepherd with a half-grown sheep slung around his neck. These economic migrants tramp, white as lepers, across the emerald carpet towards the remote promise of Californian wealth. Towards scope-rifled border patrols, salt deserts and Trumpist walls. Heavy glycerine droplets from the morning hosepipe shower slither from the sharp point of the Jesus beard. Decorative bushes have been clipped into diamond shapes.

OUR DISCUSSIONS ROAMED across the territories, but came back, time and again, to movement and stasis: the expedition and the fixed space, the writing room or cell with its books and trophies. We spoke of buildings constructed to alleviate the health of the tribe, churches, hospitals. And the connections between them in Mexico. We spoke of our own superstitious rituals for survival. And we spoke of Netley. One day I would have to visit the site.

We took a cab into town, against the advice of poolside writers disinclined to stir from their comfortable chairs, in order to inspect the José Clemente Orozco murals and to visit the Cathedral of the Assumption of Our Lady – where we discovered the waxy Santa Inocencia, a mummified martyr frothed in foam like a bride drowned in curdled milk: virginity made absolute by ravishment. Miracle cures, at the right price, are an ordinary expectation. In another alcove, another vitrine, the crucified Christ, tines of tobacco blood seeping from a chest wound, floats in narcoleptic suspension beside a set of Polaroid snapshots: fat babes, serious young girls at their first communion, married couples side by side bearing witness to the power of the effigies, in the daze of painted plaster models and blind faith.

They say that Santa Inocencia has been *dipped* in death, to varnish her unreal flesh with a tender newness, more vulnerable than that of a living child. Philip takes careful photographs for his blog. Sanctioned beggars make their pitch. The most persistent of them, eyes blank as eggs, has a green T-shirt infested with heavy metal skulls.

The cathedral, heady with incense, the hopes and fears of penitents and their candles, is an elaborate feast of gilded replicas, healing dolls, fragmentary narratives of suffering, death and resurrection. A surrealist-baroque terminus of smoky superstitions and images exploded out of primitive texts and forbidden codices. This is the point in my journey, now experienced in company with someone brought up in the rituals of the faith, in silent obedience, when the doctrine of 'living with buildings' is put to the test. The floating congregation of pilgrims, coming from all parts of the city, from far-flung communities beyond the borders of Mexico, mill around. Some stop to pray. Others, visibly sick, hobble, offering up their disabilities, in exchange for a spiritual lottery ticket, to a favourite saint.

OUR HOSTS WERE INFINITELY OBLIGING, arranging meals with friends and colleagues at lively local restaurants. They provided clear information and good company. And a car. Juan Manuel Franco Franco of the University of Guadalajara was as picture-smart as we were casual: a trim silver beard, blue jacket, pale blue shirt with red tie, silver pen in pocket. His nicely pressed jacket sleeves were an inch too long. Claudia, his vivacious wife, was in red top and black leather jacket, with a dark sweep of hair.

I like this couple, their novelty, and the evident affection and respect between them. They were always smiling, amused by our difference, interested in our strange stories and ready to facilitate or anticipate outlandish requests. That we should, for example, find time to visit the village of Teuchitlán, about an hour's drive from Guadalajara. A village between the mountains and a long shallow lake. A setting that invoked the heated, migrainous, pre-convulsive weather systems of D. H. Lawrence's lake-dwelling primitivists from *The Plumed Serpent*. Behind the village was Los Guachimontes, a series of recently excavated 2,000-year-old stepped pyramids, heaped layers of stone and turf. This expedition was the culmination of my brief Mexican visit. And the manifestation of a theory that, unlike Lawrence, I had no valid method of articulating, no form to carry the burden of contradictions, impulses and fertile ignorance.

Before the car journey – plumes of grey-white smoke from agribiz hangars behind filling stations and a stopover restaurant by the lake, where we borrowed binoculars to watch herons and pelicans from beneath a faded Coca-Cola awning – Juan Manuel took us to Tlaquepaque, an enclave of artists and artisans absorbed into the outer spill of Guadalajara. We sat, through the suspension of afternoon, hazy with drink and diffused sunlight, at a long table in an enclosed courtyard behind the studio of Manuel Ramirez Martinez.

Lawrence speaks about 'a sort of suppressed, tranced

intensity, singing to the inner mystery ... the infinite room that lies inside the axis of our wheeling space.' The tumblers of raicilla, a fierce mountain spirit, illegally brewed, might have endorsed the experience, but it was already immanent in the resting, the stillness, the table laid with baskets of bread like grainy, edible stones. And the bitter sharp oranges we were instructed to suck. Manuel's son, an otherworldly, red-headed presence, undisturbed by our intrusion, eyes focused on some remote point, above and beyond us, rocked quietly and steadily in a hammock-net of coloured strings. Chickens scratched around our feet. The walls of the courtyard were hung with gourds and found objects, objects that had found themselves and were in no way presented as decoration, or a display of the Mexican artist's perspicacity in catching them.

We drank. Time yawned. There was an amiable balance in this. Between moving, imagining the trip to the mountain village to bring back the bottles of raicilla, distilled fermentation of the agave plant, and being where we were, elbows on table, leaning against the wall of bones and branches and feeling them grow. And grow into our fingers and veins. Juice of the small orange. Another slug of raicilla. Intricate patterns of afternoon shadows. This subtle light remembers the transit through the cool interior shade of the studio, where Manuel's paintings have an ex-voto charge of gratitude for life, captured and refined epiphanies, disasters averted or survived. In this secret place, off a drowsy siesta street of artists and craftsmen, we have stopped. We are in remission: drinking, recalling other journeys and projecting future quests without stirring a muscle, lifting a leg, putting one step in front of another.

'The whole experience passed into timelessness,' Philip recalled. But it did *not* pass, that was the essence of the afternoon: the experience shimmered and held. The bottle passed. The hammock swung. The yard was a workspace, somewhere to eat and rest and dream. The red-haired boy's net pendulum rocked more and more slowly like a cancelled wave. His disembodied gaze, when he looked through us, seemed like an elective strabismus, an undeceived intensity. All the eyes of Tlaquepaque were like that now, the night vision of cats or feral dogs. They saw through flesh and motive: a street photographer we met and the painter, Manuel, who might have been assessing our potential for an ex-voto portrait, but who couldn't quite decide which misfortune should strike us down.

The courtyard, tilted and slanted by intoxication, by the sharpness of the segments of orange, was open to the sky. We were inside, hidden away, but the enclosure was also a kitchen, a playground and a gallery. The boy reminded me of one of Soutine's pastry cooks. He had that beautiful everyday otherness. The ears. And the black tar-drop eyes; one confronting us, the other absent. In his hammock, he rode the waves and watched the ocean of clouds.

After the third or fourth tumbler of raicilla, I began, or so I thought, to talk some form of old Spanish, or even Nahuatl, or a bizarre Uto-Aztecan variant known only to cacti and crows. Or some deranged blend of all of the sixty-three indigenous Mesoamerican languages identified by scholars. I attempted, with thick clay tongue, to articulate a sunburst vision of migration and movement as absolute requirements for balance and wellbeing. We should never stay in one place, one building where sickness can become concentrated and find us out. Where sickness demands its sickly rituals of sacrifice, muttered prayers to unknown gods. Philip's god was the whale: that terrible whiteness. The clicking and depth-sounding mammal herds waiting for him in the Pacific Ocean, off Puerto Vallarta.

Guadalajara was seduction. Its towers and highways. Its hotels, universities and conference centres acted as magnets. Around this courtyard table, as artists and guests, we were offered some intimation of how communal life, its interactions and silences, could work. The buildings of this quarter emerged from the ground. And were of the ground. They could vanish again, if the earth shuddered. Every object was animate, living. The animal skulls on the white wall spoke to us. Dead branches vibrated. Our gathering was a necessary stage on the journey to the locus of the stepped pyramids. We walked the streets, joined by others of the neighbourhood who appeared, laughing, mid-conversation, out of nowhere, and then we settled ourselves, like a family of affectionate strangers, at a round table in a cool, palm-shaded restaurant.

THE FIRST SOUTHAMPTON ARRANGEMENT, to walk the grounds where the Royal Victoria Military Hospital at Netley once stood, was postponed. Philip had been given a firm date for the operation on his hand. I received, along with an all clear for 20 December, a portrait of the author, bare-chested, strap around neck, heavily bandaged paw lifted in brave salute like a polar explorer with digits trimmed by frostbite. It was his right hand in mirror image. The hand captured on film in the edit by Emma Matthews, for an Arena documentary, *The Hunt for Moby-Dick*, which was shot in parallel with the publication of *Leviathan*. But not, fortunately, the hand with which he made meticulous entries in his notebook.

Dupuytren's contracture, Philip said. A thick cord of tissue, under the skin of the palm, twisting the fingers into involuntary claws. The condition, maturing, did not inhibit those daily swims in Southampton Water, down the channel between demolished hospital and oil refinery. But it was hard to manoeuvre the handles of his bicycle, the writer's favoured method of covering the ground. By reputation, Dupuytren's contracture is supposed to have a Viking origin: the gripping of oars on icy oceans, the clenching of swords and axes for raids on the northern isles. Treatments for the condition include steroid injections and physical therapy.

The three-hour fasciotomy Philip underwent, involving a grafting of bone from the elbow, was stoically borne. And witnessed with open eyes. The treated part was held firm for the procedure in a giant lead hand.

For how many years after a building disappears does it retain its potency? The ability to affect our moods and movements. Do we, like the indigenous people of the Upper Amazon, journey to place ourselves in locations where time has a different register? 'I used often to pretend I believed in ghosts,' Javier Marías said. By Southampton Water, I needed to discover if those ghosts believed in me. Philip Hoare, the swimmer, was the necessary guide to a landscape of trauma, waves of pain flowing from the memory traces of the unrelieved battlefield dead. The lost Netley colonists.

AN AFFRONTED PARLIAMENT of crows, coming out of nowhere, detonate around our heads. Philip identifies a species of gull he has never previously encountered on Southampton Water. He finds a sea urchin and a witch stone. He tells me something about the communities of Shakers, the ghost tappers and hedge visionaries in the New Forest, the scattered utopians he described in *England's Lost Eden*. These were working people 'alienated by enclosure' and naked dancers led by mad prophets preaching their own immortality as they visibly faded and fell. The structures they conceived were intended for a new Jerusalem, in which the chosen few, the believers, could live out their temporary existences in perfect balance with nature. While they were persecuted, abused and left to sleep in fields and barns.

Behind us, in the waterside park, was the resistant after-glow of the vanished military hospital, the spread of its wings, and the endless runway of the corridors down which Jonathan Miller had his name character traipse, when he came to film *Alice in Wonderland* as a Victorian scrapbook of clinical practice: the icons of imperialism babbling and twitching in a purgatorial limbo.

The jetty, Royal Victoria Military Hospital, Netley, *c.* 1880.
Soldiers can be seen on the bridge in the foreground..

Philip is preternaturally alert to manifestations of the
uncanny. He is constantly swooping to dig out and capture
evidence for a museum of 'hauntings'. He speaks of the
military discipline of the hospital and the archival footage
of damaged soldiers, returned from the trenches of the First
War and made to contort and tremble for the cameras of
doctors unashamed to be producing Chaplineque silents
with no comedy. Philip described this colony, where the
maimed were denied access to sunlight and water, their
beds facing interior courtyards, as a 'concentration breed-
ing-camp for the insane'.

The sheer scale and weight of Netley, an empire within
an empire, ruled by strict hierarchies of officers who took
the best apartments for themselves, and slavey-nurses often
treated as mere perks for the doctors and required to sleep in
cramped dormitories where the doors could not be closed,
was such that the hurt soldiers, fodder of an industrial
process, casualties of economic adventurism, were obliged
to embody and perform their sickness.

The most absorbing take on this proud architecture of ruin and the unfortunates who suffered it as part of their cure – beyond Philip's compelling history, *Spike Island* – was a chapter in B. Catling's novel of possession and magic, *The Erstwhile*. Catling researched the grounds at Netley, as we did, but confirmed, when I questioned him about it: 'There is nothing there.' And then, again, after considering it. 'But of course there is. It is *all* there. It doesn't go away.'

Catling's character, a German-Jewish professor on a mission in England, to locate buried entities known as 'The Erstwhile', fallen angels expelled from the Garden of Eden (and doubtless hidden still in the New Forest), comes with a letter of introduction to the authorities at the Royal Military Hospital. Catling's book is beyond the gravity of time. This episode happens in parallel with the rise of Hitler, while a primitive crystal radio in the Bethlem Hospital in Lambeth picks up game shows from thirty years into the future.

Schumann is ferried to the pier that is no longer there, to the place where a molten spill of Impressionist orange from the chimney of the oil refinery was witnessed on the afternoon of our visit. 'The rapidly approaching cliff was indeed the Royal Military Hospital at Netley, and it made Bethlem look like a matchbox.'

Imagine the effect of that jolting landfall on the historic stretcher cases carried ashore, before they were lodged in the castle of infirmity until their deformities could be made fit for society; until they were deemed worthy of the postcards of obligation they would be required to enact. Schumann, his oils of balance pitched and shaken by a short voyage with a pair of Shakespearian clowns, remembers the footage of naked patients, shell-shocked and traumatised in every twitching movement, being displayed like a set of awful out-takes for Buster Keaton in Bedlam.

Disorientated, thrown out of kilter, the fastidious German pedant enters the central mass, the red brick abutment with its oxidised cap. No building in England so loudly realised the dialogue between health and architecture: the concept and the actuality.

'It was a museum, he thought. A great entrance hall full of the preserved and cast. It looked as if every creature that ever walked the planet was now stuffed and ornamentally hanging from the walls and corridors ... The place was festooned with the dead.'

Dripping seawater from sodden trouser cuffs, Schumann makes his hesitant advance, a Prufrock among the specimens of slaughter and medical pathology. 'Don't your patients get disturbed?' he asks.

Of course they do. That is the point. The basket cases, the locked-in neurasthenics and the vegetoid mutes must be affronted by the scale of their prison, the curtain-flapping corridors of warped logic tapped by Jonathan Miller for an encounter between a young girl of respectable family and a tribe of eccentric and impossible adults: the great and the good of Victorian England, the court of Queen Victoria, across the water, at Osborne on the Isle of Wight. Food-spattered sages dribble into their beards. Amputees, the blind and the deafened casualties of war, are posed on chairs and painted where they lie on their tight military deathbeds.

Every step takes Schumann deeper into the heart of the madness. The German professor is reminded that the truly lost, the moon-struck, flesh-clawing cannibal lunatics have been hidden away in a separate building, the notorious D Block. 'The symptoms were weird. All different but they had a common stem: cringing fear and debilitating shock.'

The pernicious building, as Schumann penetrates its satanic interior, becomes quieter. 'It was as if all sound had been absorbed elsewhere. Even their own footfall seemed muted. It produced a kind of humming inside his head.'

The swallowing of noise becomes critical. Experimental subjects are converted to frenzied movement, as the padded wards and walls start to tear themselves apart. The architecture is sick and the visiting professor, innocent of its history, succumbs. 'Their action had been shunted, transfused into every cell of every material in the room. Everything now moved like them while they remained motionless at its centre. The eye of the storm.'

IN THESE WOODS Philip found two service revolvers and many broken clay pipes with the Netley monogram, physical traces of the asylum block. He was by nature a finder. And these finds were recognised as signs. This, he said, was a significant and remarkable day: the never-before-observed passerine gulls, the fiery path across the water, the witch stone, the sea urchin, the college of crows in a bare tree. Objects confirm Philip's sense of the uncanny, fragments left behind by certain buildings or people. As I lift my camera to try to register the faintest of borders, where the broad channel of Southampton Water runs into an equally grey but unblemished sky, navigation lights come on.

We progress around the high wall, past the weathered and secured garden door, to the main entrance of what is now a police training facility specialising in counter-terrorism rehearsals. Behind the imposing desk is a panoramic vision of Netley in its pomp, sea-facing block and satellite huts. We have heard so much about the experimental treatments in D Block: insulin comas, brain-frying ECT, induced malarial fevers, hoses, ice showers and psychotropic voyages through the shallows of madness. Philip reminds me that R. D. Laing served his time here, conscripted under the old regime, as a young doctor. Relishing his role as guide, Philip points out the diamond-cut window drawings; illustrations from a demented book of hours produced by the patients. 'Lit from behind by a fluorescent strip like an advertising hoarding, they are a votive offering to the building's unquiet spirits, a talisman of the constabulary's stewardship,' he says.

A few days later, the bandages came off. Philip sent me a portrait of his wounded hand, making a teasing reference to the stigmata. A stitched scar carved across the pad to the base of the little finger, with one neat tributary, looking like a brand, the mirror image of a lower case *h*. Or the sketch of an empty chair. Perhaps one of the chairs Catling's Schumann encountered in the innermost sound-drained ward? Philip's hand was open, but it was not soliciting alms. Instead, the exposed palm was offering us a clue to the next chapter of an evolving story.

Pilgrims, Herders and Hermits

'Space should endure while time is erased.'

Javier Marías

STAYING ON THE A859, a designation that makes absolutely no sense up here in this unforgiving landscape, we pushed north from Tarbert to Stornoway, with panic in our hearts. Was there time for a diversion towards the standing stones at Callanish, with an impulsive halt to investigate one particularly seductive ruin, in a blizzard of ruins? Like a country that had been evacuated or emptied by plague. Like the terrain of H. P. Lovecraft or the rocks, cellars and sink holes of the abandoned village of Dogtown, above Gloucester in Massachusetts. A hard place where pilgrims found the true cost of settlement.

This is how it stood, and why our unsteady negotiation across a causeway of rubble, brick fragments and smashed porcelain, with twists of indestructible plastic and sodden hanks of paper, seemed so freighted with anxiety. The 4 p.m. ferry from Stornoway to Ullapool was in question. And if we didn't get off the island now, we would be held for days, through a merciless Free Presbyterian Sunday, into a new week of Atlantic storms. The Mallaig crossing had already been suspended, after a night of howling winds through the Sound of Sleat, and the 2 p.m. Tarbert ferry on which we were provisionally booked was unlikely to sail.

Steve Dilworth's *Whalebone Box.*

This roadside ruin, enticing as it was, would not receive the attention it deserved.

I had come north at the darkest time, in company with Andrew Kötting and the pinhole photographer Anthony O'Donnell (trading as Anonymous Bosch), to return a whalebone box, supposed to have healing properties, to the sculptor Steve Dilworth, a native of Hull who had settled, many years ago, on the island of Harris. Joan, Steve's wife, had received a bad diagnosis, and I felt that everything, including my book on buildings and health, should be held in suspension, until the box was carried back to the place where it had been made. It is not only humans; the objects they make, crafted from elements of undead nature, demand a setting – house, hole, shelter. What I had not expected was this terrain of abandonment and desolation.

I have never been in a place where so many buildings, and so many varieties of building, have abdicated their original function to become part of the territory. In 2009, for *Isle of Rust*, the Hebridean chapter of his *Off-Kilter* television tour of Scotland, the funeral-suited Jonathan Meades stepped out of the hire car – which immediately, as a nice visual joke, ran away from him (cue: sound effects) – to preach a painstakingly crafted eulogy on the beauty of a depopulated country at 'the end of the world'. Meades has no truck with eco-pieties or sentimental misappropriations of Gaelic culture. His lecture was a playful manifesto for a 'scrap cult': entropy expressed in the luscious wet-tongued colours – blast-furnace orange, boiled lobster pink – of corrugated iron shacks. 'Ad hoc follies,' he called them. 'A shackscape.'

This intimacy with the processes of oxidisation, rust, curling flecks of paint, aligned nicely with one of the other late manifestations of the Meades brand: his exposure as an image maker, painter and sprayer of gallery-friendly pieces. The presenter said that he had a 'hatred' of manifestos and a love of combining 'contradictory elements'. But the shed/shack/bothy/*taigh* promotion, delivered by an uncomfortably articulate witness on this boggy, rock-infested moonscape, is a manifesto of affection; a broadside fired at Bible-black fundamentalism and bogus tartan tourism. This man can feel so smart – and right – that stumbling, accidentally, into one of his sets leaves you wrestling to shut the door of some battered crime-scene caravan, while trying to paste back issues of *The Stornoway Gazette* over cobwebbed windows.

Act now! Before clipped anathemas overwhelm the unscripted perversity of the gangrene desert into which we have strayed. And through which we want to tramp, in order to unravel the enigma of the relationship between the ruins, the stone outcrops, the rocks that might be sheep, and the tribal soul and sustenance of the people who abide here. Living with these ex-buildings and near-buildings seems to be about deserting them, walking out and never returning. When a member of the family takes sick, the building is blamed. Turn away, put up another. As if the structures – turf lodges, substantial cottages, stone tents, whaling stations and fantasy castles of deer-bothering proprietors – had themselves been identified as the source of the sickness. A sickness expressed as grinding poverty and inherited malpractice. As arbitrary clearances and relocations. Better to anticipate the coming pestilence from the next remote proprietor, they said, and to keep moving. Footpaths and desire lines are soon absorbed into the landscape. Into the rain and mist. Ships wait in the harbour to carry away human cargo to a bigger and better wilderness.

Kötting has no hesitation about how to behave when confronted with the evidence of unexplained migration. Having found a seatless lavatory bowl, left out in the freezing air, where a bathroom once stood, between two unsupported walls, he drops his trousers and squats.

Lord Leverhulme, the former William Hesketh Lever of Bolton, world-moving soap magnate of Port Sunlight, and the most ambitious seigneur of the Hebridean islands, was a small, bristling person, a dynamo of neurotic energy, increasingly hard of hearing – and stone-deaf to any opinion that contradicted his own. Uxorious but driven, Leverhulme reluctantly shut his eyes for a few hours at night, but rose before dawn for a session of vigorous callisthenics, before getting down to the day's business, well ahead of his clerks and labourers. He insisted on having his bedchamber exposed – like Kötting – to the elements. It was open to the landscape, to the weather. The magnate knew that it was healthier not to be trapped indoors, at the mercy of moulds and germ cultures and the pincered bugs of nightmare that sheltered in heavy drapes and wallpaper. Architecture was the discipline most sympathetic to the Methodist plutocrat. He loved plans and models. He abhorred the native crofter and his sense of entitlement to a few yards of ancestral muck and machair, instead of becoming an adequately rewarded card-puncher in a fish factory. With a suburban bungalow.

What attracts Meades to this place is what he calls 'an aesthetic bereavement so absolute that it is a sort of insouciant anti-aesthetic.' A palette of corruption. The script for *Isle of Rust*, published in *Museum Without Walls* (2012), states: 'ESSENTIAL TO COMPOSE FRAMES THAT SHOW CORRUGATED IRON, MACHINERY, SCRAP, ETC., IN THEIR SURROUNDINGS. EMPHASISE THE CONTRAST BETWEEN NATURAL GRANDEUR AND SCRAP SQUALOR.'

But there is no contrast; out here, squalor and grandeur are synonymous. The megalithic clock of the standing stones has no more status than the adjacent grass-roofed hutch or its satellite caravan – which could be seen as the favoured dwelling. The caravan has wheels, it can roll on. Its location is arbitrary and provisional. It looks like two tin coracles welded, one on top of the other, using the abandoned house as a windbreak.

Steve Dilworth, when we found his property and settled

Ruins, Isle of Lewis.

ourselves around the hospitable table, told us that some of the wealthiest and most successful native landowners chose to keep their heads down in caravans, while collecting rents from a raft of desirable properties. Restored or plausibly Bauhaused, picture-windowed investments on the Atlantic side of Harris went, in the season, for between £2,000 and £4,000 a week.

What struck me, listening to Meades as he waxed lyrical about shackscapes and the aesthetics of exposed corrugated iron, were the medical metaphors. Buildings, without inhabitants or purpose, have found their sickness vocation: metal is metastasised flesh. 'These scapes are beautiful in the way that a lupus is beautiful.' The presenter talks of 'mould on fruit'. When the camera moves close enough to linger over the patina of damage, Meades contrasts roofless houses with 'decaying meat, scar tissue, amputations, or anatomical freaks'. It is like identifying the traumas of the Royal Victoria Military Hospital at Netley from an examination of the demolished jetty, the odd stones found in the woods. 'This is the great outdoors as it might have been conceived by hothouse poets of the darkest indoors.'

AS WE TRAVELLED NORTH, I became mesmerised by the desolation of scored lines across the snowcapped hills, lines that could never be identified as natural features: three-billion-year-old extrusions of gneiss, glacial detritus or the vestigial walls of animal pens that had evolved into ridges among the grey-white, chlorophyll-drained bracken.

Between 1818 and 1886, sporting landlords fenced off 50,000 acres of Lewis for sheep farming and deer runs. Punitive clearances, with the crofters regarded as a native nuisance, stubborn beyond reason, decanted the workable land of the west and engineered survivalist clusters among the rock inlets of the east. A terrain so bleak and stony that it was not worth keeping beasts on it. Those who settled constructed *feannagan* or lazy beds; patches of earth no

larger than a kitchen table laboriously built up on mat-
tresses of cut turf. Dwellings were shared with animals. The
dry-stone walls of rudimentary bunkers were roofed with
turf. Meanwhile, Lord Leverhulme, the amateur architect
with funds to indulge his self-serving utopianism, motored
over the islands – as we were doing – and pronounced the
ground 'not fit for kaffirs'. He twinned paternalistic notions
of managed fish harvests (and dairy herds and cottages for
grateful workers) with Conradian ventures in the Congo
and the Solomon Islands.

The curse held. Isolated homesteads were broken and
deserted. Sheds, looking more like slaughterhouses, or processing plants with nothing left to process, thrived. They
became blue slate Community Co-Op trading posts and
tastefully arranged display zones for newly fashionable –
'infused with sugar kelp' – gin distillers, flagging up the
quinine element in tonic water as a palliative against seasonal midge-bite malaria.

But the Hebridean houses, the homes ... roofless, win-
dowless, stripped and gutted ... they remained: markers
and memorials. You might find a single slender wall with its
roughcast dressing, solitary aperture – and a crack running
into the earth like a lightning bolt from the chimney.

On the islands, it takes time to notice that a family has
disappeared and its property is available for redistribution.
The attendant shed will be in better shape, maybe with a
pair of salvageable bicycles still leaning against it. And there
will be a drunken, lopsided caravan like some part of a container shipment washed up on the shingle. It's not always
an enforced expulsion. Steve told us that the last occupant
would frequently just walk away, peat on the fire, Bible on
the table. Going, going, gone. And never heard from again:
Canada, New Zealand, London.

I TRIED TO INTERROGATE Dilworth for BBC 2's *Late Show*
in 1991. His sculpture, *Hanging Figure*, a sinister presence

made from human bones, calf meat, formaldehyde, sodium fluoride, hair and sea-grass, swung from a butcher's hook beside the dentist's chair in which the reluctant interviewee sprawled. It would have been easier to squeeze a coherent response from the suspended, gently revolving creature. My sense, back then, was of an artist recovering votive objects for a tribe that never existed. A man in a house that was also store, workshop, home, museum. And centripetal table for hospitality, dinner and conversation through the dark winter days. The health of any human, after many adventures and detours, is confirmed by choosing to live – if such a choice is possible – in the good place. A place with no interest in, or sympathy for, our feeble interventions.

Steve scavenged and scoured. Boiler-suited like Churchill in wartime, gloved and scarfed, he laboured through long winters, chiselling, grinding and carving. He made throwing objects for writers and academics who would never hunt, and larger pieces, caskets and containers of trapped animal spirits, for a varied constituency of worldwide collectors. And kists, storm charms, such as the cored dolerite with the glass phial of seawater Steve contrived for Robert Macfarlane, before the Cambridge academic sailed from Stornoway to St Kilda. When the inevitable storm came, the kist was to be thrown over the side: the gift ungiven. As my whalebone box had to return, unjourneyed, narrative subsumed, to its place of origin.

The white house in which Steve lived with Joan, and where his daughters grew up, a restored and improved, slate-roofed, sea-facing block, with its diminishing store of calm water in plastic bottles, its squashed owls and anvil of whalebone, was an enlarged version of the sealed container the sculptor put into my hands. The house was a functioning machine. The box was an animal battery and a charm against future diseases. It could not prevent them, but it provided an object to be carried, struggled with, in the plotting of walks and pilgrimages of restitution.

After trying to discover and decode a disguised track across the mountains, a solitary walk undertaken as part of *The Old Ways* (2012), Macfarlane found that his tired feet were guided to Dilworth's door – for a necessary debriefing, yarning session, food and drink, books, music, warmth and just sitting in silence. All carried through in good humour. 'A shaman who took himself seriously,' Macfarlane wrote, 'would be insufferable.' But a shaman who does not take himself seriously is not a shaman. His sickness vocation is misplaced. The clowning of the shaman is a weapon.

On the studio shelf, as Macfarlane reveals, between an ivory tusk and a jar labelled '4,000-Year-Old Storm Water', Steve keeps the last box of Pick 'n' Mix sweets from the closing sale at Woolworths in Tarbert.

IN SEPTEMBER 2017, I saw Steve and Joan at the opening of his latest exhibition, *Off the Rock*, at the Pangolin London gallery in King's Place, York Way. Friends and art casuals processed around the chosen pieces. Joan was looking well, comfortable in the wash of meeting and greeting. I knew that she was undergoing regular doses of chemotherapy at the hospital in Stornoway, as well as paracentesis procedures (the tapping of excess fluids through a hollow candle or cannula), but there was no evidence of it. We talked about this being the moment to bring the whalebone box north. And Steve said that they were off, right after the show, for a brief holiday in the warmth of the South of France. The plan was to get together with Meades at l'Unité d'habitation for a special meal. It never happened. There were complications with hotel reservations and an attempt to shift them out to another place on the periphery. Too much hassle. Steve decided to leave Marseille out of his plans.

TIME SHRINKS. Mortality bites. I heard about Joan. Her health was an important part of my memory of the good place where the Dilworth family lived. I had become very comfortable with the companionship of the whalebone box. It would hurt to return it, so the moment had arrived. To delay the parting for a week or two, I carried the box upriver, church by pilgrim church along the Thames.

I halt the car, sleet blanking the windscreen, where I always park in Dorchester-on-Thames. Inky tendrils are running through the accumulated grease of the road. Further down the lane, a necessary trudge of reconnaissance, I managed to identify the landing place on the mirrored ice of the Thame where we beached the canoe, when I paddled here from Oxford with Brian Catling. His neck was locked in spasm and he was thirsty for the pub, the Fleur de Lys.

'The light music of whisky falling to glasses made an agreeable interlude,' as Joyce would say. We enjoyed the respite and the inward glow, before we admitted that the canoe was never going to fit on the roof of the unfamiliar Mini driven by Brian's wife, who had in any case just passed her test. The situation was rescued by a colleague from the Ruskin School of Art. Kevin Slingsby lived in the village, in a house near the Abbey. He was proud to announce that he taught the 'almost extinct' skill of stone lithography. Our canoe was gathered up and later delivered by suitable vehicle to a riverside property in Oxford.

Now, when I carried the box across the road to the Abbey, my first station would be beneath the processional cross, made on commission by Catling, as a memorial for Slingsby, and engraved with a private dedication. The cross was long and slender, short-armed. 'The surface marks of its cutting, welding and forging act as expressive signatures of human pain and endurance,' Catling glossed. He was determined to respect, in his own fashion, 'traditional elements of Northern European Christian art'. The stainless steel stem is taller than the door in the wall behind it. The processional cross is placed in relation to the red-earth

Bright Rising by Rebecca Hind.

colour of a recovered fourteenth-century cross in a recessed
arch, and a crucifixion fresco. Catling's slender carrying
pole has been attached to a cross made in the same proportions as the one in the arch above it. Sun and moon, the
heavenly disks associated with the rituals of this site, hang
over the three plant-like figures depicted in the crucifixion
scene.

The Abbey church has its rumoured hauntings, its
unquiet tenants ready to perform their traditional role: it
is a place of pilgrimage. The dormitories are gone along
with the crusts for weary travellers. A determined effort has
been made to democratise the space and make it useful,
somewhere for children and for community exhibitions.
Dilworth's whalebone box, once it is set down, establishes
a rapport with the other monuments and with the Jesse tree
window. The yellowing horn of the box-battery manufac-
tures its own internal light, setting this object apart from
the candled tomb-sleepers, the fired colour in the leaded
jigsaw of stained glass, and that luminous panel, *Bright
Rising*, painted in watercolour for the reredos of the Lady
Chapel by Rebecca Hind.

Hind's liquid projection, a quietist addition to this
cluttered, over-curated church, where surviving or restored
relics associated with almost forgotten beliefs argue
with plastic toys, pamphlets and promotions, is the only

artwork that references *this* place. It was made here and set here, a subtle veil of wash and weather dissolving the barrier of the church wall and floating the attentive visitor out into the landscape, the water meadows. We rise above the Sinodun Hills and remember the late paintings of Paul Nash, the foreshortening of vision as he looked at the sacred loci through binoculars from his sickbed on Boar's Hill.

Living in part of the rectory, behind the Abbey, Rebecca Hind was a daughter of the church. Her father, Canon Stanley Hind, moved the family around various parishes in the north of England. She was the widow of Kevin Slingsby, our Dorchester rescuer, the artist who succumbed to incurable motor neurone disease. Two years later Rebecca's father died. And the blows continued to fall. Hind's brother Martin was taken by cancer. Now, at a time when her mature work was being exhibited and winning new admirers, Rebecca received her own cruel diagnosis. That every remaining grain of her time was measured.

SNOW FELL HEAVILY in the night. The box, left unattended in the car, was letting its weather out with a vengeance, in preparation for the road north. The return to Harris. Buses were skewed across the steep hill in Headington as I drove out of Oxford. A few miles further and I had to climb from the car to help push a convoy of stalled and slithering motors, one by one, over the brow of a blocked dual carriageway.

The miles unravelled. After we crossed the border, I tried to keep a photographic record of the box's journey. An anvil rock with a man-made cave. A winter pond cropped with reeds like phantom wheat in an abandoned quarry. Fractal patterns in thick ice, trapped air bubbles.

Then a sudden chill in the darkness of Glen Coe's compacted history, the silence of expulsion and blood feud. And that granite boulder on its plinth at Ballachulish: a blinded

Hanging Figure by Steve Dilworth.

featureless head set in memory of the executed Jacobite James Stewart. James of the Glen. A sacrificial victim hanged for the murder of the factor Colin Ray Campbell, a crime of which he was almost certainly innocent.

Stewart, a man of the wrong dispensation, was swiftly condemned after a show trial with a jury of Campbell placemen and a Campbell judge. The assassination, bullet in the back, and the judicial execution belonged to the period of evictions, land clearances, property seizures and 'pacification' that followed the defeat of the Jacobite uprising at Culloden in 1746.

Coming on this still haunted memorial by accident, while processing the whalebone box, giving it a sniff of the choppy waters under the bridge, and out at the mouth of Loch Leven, was a useful preparation for our approach to Steve Dilworth – and a direct invocation of Dilworth's

Hanging Figure. A reminder that his sculptural practice was never made outside the reach of native cultural memory. The chained Jacobite corpse, left to swing on a thirty-foot gibbet for three years, as a grotesque public sculpture, visible to passengers on the ferry across the loch, achieved the exposure Dilworth was careful to avoid. His *Hanging Figure*, neither male nor female, calf meat and sea-grass, would have been hidden, if the funding had been achieved, inside a hollowed-out Harris boulder. With no legend. No explanation. And few witnesses.

Crows pecked at the tarry traces. Robert Louis Stevenson took the bones of the tale, the Appin Murder, and reconfigured them around Alan Breck Stewart, the foster son of the hanged man, for *Kidnapped*. Thereby 'improving' the narrative and keeping the myth alive. Anonymous butchers, skilled in autopsy arts, knitted the rotting flesh with tendons and sinews of wire and rope to keep the death-moulded piece 'alive'. Until, it is thought, a simple-minded local man tore the remnants down and flung them in the loch.

AT KYLE OF LOCHALSH we broke off, before crossing the bridge to Skye, to search for the public toilets featured in Kötting's round-Britain saga, *Gallivant*. He shot a nice little cameo with the prize-winning attendant (hygiene operative, curator); a man who gloried in godly cleanliness and a worldwide display of postcards from satisfied customers. This civic amenity, decommissioned in so many lesser places, was built to service travellers leaving the mainland for the islands.

But, much more than this, we wanted to locate the Skye hermit. Here was an independent spirit who struck us as a significant interpreter of difference, the one who could prepare us for the way that Hebridean folk treated buildings: as tents, yurts, temporary conveniences on the great journey. As the Sami, the reindeer herders of the north, crossing vast tracts of forest and frozen lake, find cut poles leaning, ready and waiting, against a tree, and make a one-night camp. Carrying with them, on their sledge, coverings, skins, cooking pots, fire sources.

Andrew encountered the hermit, a ripe personage who came over to the public toilets once a week, before picking up his money and supplies, to strip and lather at the basin, a thorough rinse and scrape. The man wasn't for conversation. He kept on the move, before mortality, the will to sickness hidden in any fixed location, could find him out. Say nothing. Rise early. Walk until the sun drops. Use bus shelters, unsecured caravans and public toilets as staging posts, sanctuaries on a circular pilgrimage.

Dilworth told us about one wanderer (no property, no papers) who kept off a treacherous diagnosis, overwintering in the bitterest conditions, by wedging a walking stick under the hot-air blower in the well-maintained Hebridean public convenience that he made his seasonal home.

IN THE FINAL DARKNESS of the far north, on a night glittering with more stars than I had seen in years, I recognised the white house, behind its masking fuchsia hedge, in the rocky settlement at Geocrab. We had picked our way along the single-track coast road out of Tarbert, through the inlets and the junked buses favoured for occupation over cottages and bungalows, while avoiding unconcerned sheep.

I knocked but Steve was already waiting, with Joan inside. Nothing had changed and everything had changed. The *Hanging Figure* had a passport now. It had been acquired by a death collector in Chicago and shipped out. But the whalebone box, my penance and goad, was home. It had never quite been settled that Steve would accept it, but he took the burden, immediately, from my hands and set it down on a window ledge among smaller pieces, stones and eggs and feathers. The charge of the box, its natural radio therapy, was needed. The reservoir of calm water, kept in the cold studio in a plastic bottle, was running low.

Discussing the protocol of giving, Steve insisted that parting with an object should hurt the donor. Otherwise the gesture carried no force. For an offering to be effective – calming a storm or countering viral insult – it must feel like a self-inflicted amputation. The thing passed on diminishes the substance of the one making the offer. This is no light matter. 'There are two kinds of offering,' Robert Macfarlane wrote, 'placatory and sacrificial.'

WE DROVE NEXT MORNING to St Clement's Church at Rodel. Dilworth, in dark glasses, sitting beside Andrew, gave us the stories of every house we passed. So many islanders had walked away. Wealthier folk from the mainland were moving in; they were trawling for images, mapping vanished pathways, community singing, feeding blogs and bottling their own blends of hipster gin.

The box sat in its pre-ordained place on the stone flags of the church floor. In the tower, denied access to the roof, we found a chamber with a tin tray set to catch the drips. Stone light fused in a white haze from a narrow aperture shaped like a candle. Dilworth, preoccupied, stood off. In the photographs of that day, he is just out of focus, softened, inward, on the point of dissolving into otherness.

Coming across to his house that morning, we told Steve, we noticed a disorientating hallucination: as we drove alongside a frozen loch, it appeared that water was flowing both ways at once, that we were being *followed* by tidal reflections like a storm-wash of branches or fallen leaves, while the drift of the ice went the other way. The effect was as vertigo inducing as zooming in while tracking out.

Emerging from the car with box and spade, where a tumbled cemetery spilled into sand dunes, we coincided with a small burial party. It was tactful to make a wide detour to the shore, where our elongated shadows fell across the beach in the direction of Taransay.

The box was well buried, in a secret spot, with the

Burial of the whalebone box, Isle of Harris.

expectation of being recovered one day, enigmatic but undated, like the walrus ivory chessmen of Lewis, found near Uig in 1831. After so much discussion, the interment was swift and easy. The dog walker at the tide's edge and the solitary landscape-collector with the tripod, tramping south, would barely have noticed our sombre group, silhouetted against the setting sun.

It was easy to forget how Catholic Steve's art had always been, the religion of his youth now turned towards heresy, the manufacture of relics for his own theology. With a Capuchin bias towards burial and mummification.

The day was perfect. And the mineral sky clear with a few gauzy clouds scraping along the wave contours of low hills. 'There's a good chance the ferry will be suspended tomorrow,' Steve said. 'The winds are going to get up overnight. You might be stuck here for weeks.'

That couldn't happen. The placement of the box was the resolution of a very long story. I needed to be back in London, deadlines of all sorts were closing on me. But Dilworth, the maker, the craftsman, had acquired the traditional island skill of *speuradaireachd,* or weather forecasting by remembering, by understanding the rites of blessing and cursing. He also, like many sculptors and artists stuck for hours in cold sheds, listened to the radio.

WE FINISHED with another memorable meal at the long, softly lit table, a well-endowed bouillabaisse (to compensate for the dinner in Marseille that Steve never made), and a spectacular Pavlova pudding that Joan had stayed at home to prepare. There was a constantly renewed supply of good wine, and a bottle of home-produced gin brought by Steve's neighbour, John Maher (of the Buzzcocks), now a photographer of freakishly lit Hebridean shelters and shacks. John wanted to meet Andrew Kötting, whose films he knew and relished. Anthony, back in the Preston days, was a big Buzzcocks fan. He *lived* on the road to Manchester. He was there at twenty-one of the gigs. 'Another stalker!' John replied. They got on, right away.

Over the first few bottles, Steve narrated, between pre-emptive coughs of laughter, selected episodes from his revised autobiography: up to the age of fourteen, he had been a promising mathematician, something of a prodigy. Then he fell for poetry, producing screeds of stuff that he sent to a famous figure of the day: Brian Patten, he thinks. They corresponded. Steve took up art, that was where the bohemians were to be found, girls with black stockings and panda eyes. But already, this was a shift, another chapter in an unresolved quest: Steve was in an established relationship and living in Blackheath.

He didn't have much to offer at the interview in Maidstone, crumbling plaster pieces in an old briefcase and a few unconvinced drawings. One of the panel recognised something of the madness, the conviction, and persuaded the others to let him in on licence. Steve took to the woods with a book. Another more responsible student from South London was deputed to find him and bring him back: a certain Brian Catling played the Henry Morton Stanley role. They hit it off, both having broader and more singular interests and fetishes than the course allowed. They made objects, they wrote. They hunted. And, above all, they took the time to immerse themselves in the science, ethnography, literature, landscape, painting, crime and perversion of the past. They knew how to use museums.

My remarking on a set of golf clubs, out beside the trays of green apples, the racks of wine and muddy wellington boots in the porch, set Joan off. She told me that she enjoyed nine holes on the windswept links on the Atlantic side, usually with a girlfriend. Sometimes with Steve – who could be over-competitive. Unsurprisingly.

A Londoner once, a Holloway girl, Joan gave the appearance of not being quite sure how she had landed among the gneiss outcrops of the Pleistocene in Geocrab. But being amused at the idea. And ready to make the best of it, with irregular excursions promised elsewhere, time off for good behaviour. Like weeks in her hometown, staying in borrowed chambers at the Inner Temple, walking to evening pubs around Fleet Street and Carey Street, seeing friends.

In the eddies and swirls of tale telling, an established local tradition, Joan revealed that she was a record-breaking touch typist and an awesome taker of shorthand. She wasn't much of a reader these days, because previous experience as a meticulous and unforgiving copy-editor (the kind we all dread) made the negotiation with print too slow. She couldn't see the words for the rogue apostrophes, the misplaced commas. Steve, on the other hand, devoured libraries, in a free-ranging, truffling sort of way. Andrew said that he liked me to send him copies of my books with the pages in which he appeared clearly numbered on the flyleaf.

And then, after the gin and the resinous smoke, Kötting began to sing, a cod operatic turn of his own devising, signalling that it was probably time to go home. The scraping back of chairs and slamming of doors usually followed.

'Alone on a hill lives a man with no arms and no legs,' he bellowed, with appropriate gestures.

The chorus, never previously heard, came back at once. From Joan. In tune. Vibrato. 'He has no arms, he has no legs.'

Then Andrew again. Bass. Resonant. 'Where does he live? Where does he live?'

Joan: 'Alone on the hill, alone on the hill.'

Ridiculous and magical. This unlikely duet was what we had travelled to Harris to hear. Joan, her story completed, was free to join with, and to elevate Andrew's operatic nonsense.

Stumbling on icy steps, Anthony – who was used, at home in St Leonards-on-Sea, to taking his sundowner gin by the thimble not the wellington boot – lurched and swayed, gone in the legs, staggering up the road to the parked car.

The wind Steve had promised was getting up nicely, plucking at slates, tearing the lids from tin shacks, tilting abandoned coaches. Across from our cottage, the farmer was out with his lantern, grabbing at flightless chickens hurled into the air, ready to nail them to their perches.

Crofters on Lewis, we were informed, had rights to the land but not the buildings. The land was their health, their inheritance. The strength bequeathed by distant generations. Buildings gave them temporary shelter. The most important structures belonged to outsiders, damaged folk from elsewhere, drying out, putting themselves together, stalking the rockscape and the shore.

There are bright windows now in the solid darkness, pools of light where groups gather to sing or talk or drink. The tempest has escaped from the buried box.

Spitalfields: Scintilla

'This is how we will remember light.'

B. Catling

BURSTING THROUGH HEAVY DOORS, across the flags of the Palladian portico, between the great Tuscan columns and down wide stone steps, needle heels chipping at fossils, towards … banked lighting rigs and cameras. A synchronised troop of hyper-hyper dancers with dangerous white smiles.

The monumental Hawksmoor church, this perplexing architectural and cultural conundrum, a Portland stone temple emptied of the district's dead, had gone over: definitively. It was, for this Christmas Special, for this season and forever afterwards, showbiz. And witnessed by millions. Tagged and blitzed and bothered on anti-social media. As a set, a suitable backdrop – black tails flying, hair flying, starched white shirts, red skirts belling out, spinning, shaping, skating across the polished marble of the nave, the performance floor cleared of pews and chairs (and ghosts) – for television royalty, for *Strictly Come Dancing*.

They decorated the side aisles with uniformly conical Christmas trees frosted in silver, dozens of small pulsing bulbs. I remembered a photograph from Iceland that Brian Catling showed me, when I visited him in Oxford to inspect the hundreds of images he had filed on his device, of the paintings and preparations and journeys of Rebecca Hind. This was a cemetery, a dwarf forest locked in hard snow, where all the memorial crosses were draped with lights: winter solstice like a day of the dead in Las Vegas. A celebration of the unseen and unforgotten in a funerary allotment planted against dark mountains, volcanoes and migrating cloud continents.

In front of the altar, a mixed choir had been positioned; four strict lines of scarlet-robed parishioners exploited as backing singers. If it had been possible to track through the strictly dancing couples and to freeze on the choir, the formal arrangement would have achieved a very different resonance. Above those forty white heads, now strobing like candle flames, was a watercolour triptych in a dark wood frame, part of the furniture of the older theatre of Christ Church, Spitalfields. The triptych was assembled and lifted into place by Rebecca Hind, for an exhibition in 2010.

Scintilla: the glittering speck was commissioned to respond to discrete but interpenetrating acts of Christian worship: Life (Birth), Death (Crucifixion), Resurrection (Ascension). The triptych was hung with associated works in a Christ Church show, open to the public and due to be struck in December 2010. But the three key pieces remain to this day unpromoted, status obscure; a subtle but balance-shifting addition to the essential fabric of the building. A response from a woman, very sure of the risks she was taking, to the overwhelming gender dominance – tradition, politics, patronage – of Hawksmoor's masculine master-piece. The architect heaps order of architecture on order of architecture to achieve a verticality that seems impos-sible, but inevitable. His church is a vast London sculpture moored alongside Spitalfields Market.

In contrast, the arterial flow within Hind's paintings was achieved horizontally, on the floor of the studio, tilting a secure base in order to manoeuvre 'accident', through strategic spillage and deft interventions with a large brush.

Rebecca Hind at work.

The *Scintilla* triptych is a mediating Christ Church presence, in necessary dialogue with the elegant whites and golds of the stripped Hawksmoor interior (far from his original plan) and the leaded jigsaw of stained glass above the altar, a fractured and pious orthodoxy.

The sculptural worthies, solid ghosts on either side of the reredos, act like curtain holders revealing the inner secrets of a mystery cult. Sir Robert Ladbroke, chained in worldly honours, the cloaked and wigged 'father of the City', in wrinkled tights, pinched at the crotch and dressing to the right, is framed in marble at the door of a pyramid sepulchre. Ladbroke represents the power of investment and Christian charity, while keeping his back to the shimmering panels of watercolour light. Sir Edward Peck, on the south side, is egg-eyed and smirking at death, attended by two fat cherubs.

When I heard from Catling that Rebecca was ill, invaded by the Other – not 'dying', because that would imply acceptance of the verdict, a failure of nerve, and a 'final' period of unfulfilled projects and diminishing pleasures so real that they could still be touched and tasted – my blind instinct was to walk out of the door and down to Spitalfields. To position myself in front of those luminous paintings, the *Scintilla* triptych. To enter into some sort of crude negotiation. I thought of Ed Dorn's plain statement in *Recollections of Gran Apacheriá*: 'The original monuments of perception/ are the play of light/ through the wall's membrane.' Hind's screens dissolved that stone membrane, as well as the barriers of dogma and established privilege. Distinctions between interior and exterior, observer and observed, were abolished. The east wall folded suddenly back, as if on a hinge, cleaning the floodgates of perception, and opening the masonry of the church to city and sky.

Every free afternoon that came my way, if I could get down there before they locked the doors, I climbed the familiar steps, crossed the portico, removed my cap, nodded to the woman at the desk, cricked my neck in acknowledgement of the restored magnificence – absolute, but somehow hollow, like the interior of a fabulous cake made from plaster of Paris – and took my seat in the front row, staring at and through and out of Hind's watercolours.

Effects I struggle to calibrate were happening in the arched 'Death' panel. They were brought about, in part, by the imposed Christ Church lighting scheme, pairs of high spots casting intrusive shadows and colluding with darkness from the shape of the twin pillars on either side of the central arch. Behind the white thread of a lightning strike, like the profile of a river, tipped paint snaking across the studio floor, there appeared an elongated profile, inside a floating outline like a grail cup. An unintended invader, barely registering, but certainly there. The watercolours, built up in layers, now moved like retreating, breathing veils.

There were no postcards available and the folded booklet from the *Scintilla* exhibition in 2010, with the fine introductory tribute by Catling, was not on display. The Indian lady, the embedded custodian, found a key to the store cupboard and dug out a copy for me. She asked, as she had every afternoon that week, if I liked music. And she told me, as she had every afternoon that week, that Handel played on the church's mighty organ. We would have the same conversation tomorrow. I persisted: the paintings were alive, they were not sickening or diminishing in candlepower, they gave something to the baroque building, and they challenged it. The solution to my difficulties with architecture and health was in front of me. As yet I could make nothing of it. I would return. 'Thus the scintilla becomes a synecdoche for creation,' Hind said, 'vital but intangible, negligible yet enormous.'

Illustrating the obituary in the *Yorkshire Post* – 'Rebecca Hind, royal artist' – is a portrait of a smiling Englishwoman, firmly planted, northern, and happy to pose for a moment in front of a chopped segment of the Christ Church triptych. Attached to the curve of her scoop-necked, belted dress is a pagan clump of plant life, like mistletoe or broccoli from the market or a hank of plucked corn. Or some strange marine creature, an affectionate familiar. A Lammas offering for the Autumn equinox?

This confident woman offers a wicked expression of delight in what has been accomplished. The evidence is there behind her back. Hind is fifty-two-years-old. 'The future,' said Althusser, 'lasts forever.'

I HAD TO CONVINCE MYSELF that repeated journeys towards a screen of watercolours in a Hawksmoor church served a purpose. But too many after-images of a frantic and fading metropolis were carried with me to the chair where I would sit, sometimes for a few minutes, sometimes much longer, waiting for the thing to happen. Before another brief conversation with the unblinking custodian at her table of papers. I knew this woman now as Ava, but every nod of acknowledgement was the first. 'Do you like music?'

On my walk from Hackney I noticed a fluffy pink lady who had her spaniel rigged to a device in matching pink, so that as the pampered captive struggled in her wake, he was forced to perform a set of increasingly desperate push-ups. The rear legs were useless, abbrieviated stumps. The wheels and the stumps left twin tracks across the grass.

The density of mendicants, some authentically ruined, some careerist, increased as I passed under Shoreditch railway bridge. The usual troop of excited iPhone record-ists were trophying the latest wall art revisions. There are always film crews not filming, but taking over the pavement. Special police with shaven heads and heavily tattooed arms, like Ben Stokes or David Beckham, were packing their ve-hicles with the latest weaponry and armour.

A half-naked man shawled in a grey blanket, and trail-ing a moulting teddy bear, crossed to the other side. A community cop engaged with the woman bivouacked in the doorway of a Tesco Metro. They are old friends.

The badged performer leading a party of Ripper tour-ists paused outside the façade of a Jack London dormitory staffed by nuns. 'There was no fog on Ripper nights,' he pronounced. 'Men and women were not allowed to sleep together. The last victim, Mary Kelly, was alleged to have stayed in this refuge.'

The subterranean public lavatory outside Christ Church has been converted into a hipster gin bar. 'Bathtub Gin and Rumbullion' is on offer at a cocktail price. 'Summer Gimlet': £8 a shot. 'Bathtub gin navy strength with a dash of absinthe' for landlubbers with nautical beards.

A smart black lady in a trouser suit and heels gave me the good news, without looking into my bloodshot eyes: 'Jesus loves you!' She was bumped aside by an agitated cook in a striped blue apron screaming at her fist phone: 'There's no mice in black puddings!'

The iron gates are still open. As I navigate the steps down which the *Strictly* dancers exploded, I consider the interventions of the two women I associate with Christ Church; one, conceptual (and playful) – and the other, delivered and in place. The veil of light from Rebecca Hind and the earth burial of the whole structure as proposed by Carol Williams, when she reacted against a perceived malignancy, a barrier to the health, social and spiritual, of this district. A grassed and planted mound – like a grander version of the bandstand elevation at Arnold Circus – to offer respite, and new prospects of city and river.

The inhumation Williams proposed had a pedigree. It might send Christ Church spiralling back through time. I thought of the mysterious Navan Fort (or Emain Macha) in County Armagh; a circular hilltop enclosure, inside which there is a mound and a ring barrow. Archaeological evidence suggests that a timber structure was filled with stones, then deliberately burnt to the ground. And covered with earth to create the mound that can still be seen. The Fort stands at the centre of a complex of other sites, as well as a ritual pool and a lake from which numerous votive offerings have been recovered. Flooded and buried, Hawksmoor's church has the strength to become an epic version of Dilworth's box.

I UNDERSTOOD FROM WALKS we shared, to the Olympic 'parkland' in Stratford, and to Tilbury and Stanford-le-Hope, that Williams was looking closely at play areas, sponsored plantings on brownfield sites, virgin estates, attempts to balance ex-industrial environments with failed or successful regeneration plans. She had a new and challenging job, hired by a friend to improve, restore and rebalance, the energies of a housing project, just outside New York City in Yonkers. Carol, as I understood it, was a consultant, a spy for truth, stalking the perimeters of the given territory as an initiator of practical suggestions – and a person permitted to hold free and wide-ranging discussions, on equal terms (thanks to their shared history), with her patron. But now, as had so often happened in the past, Carol's involvement with an actual project, built around dreams of good

housing and health, played out alongside my wilder speculations and retrievals from London rambles.

In 1998 Williams published *Bringing a Garden to Life*,
a book of practical advice and instruction freighted with
the suggestion that garden work, intimate engagement
with any small patch of ground, would counter the force of
'hurricanes, floods, family crises, and deer depredations.'
The retreat or oasis of an enclosed physic garden is a good
model. 'It is known that people who are ill have regained
health in the garden; broken hearts have been made whole.
But I think it is not the garden so much as the gardening
that performs these miracles.'

A passage I marked in Carol's book registered one point
of disagreement, something to debate as we walked, appreciating the way that nature swallows and dresses wrecked
motorbikes on the foreshore and provides habitat for crabs
and plants thriving on pollution within the rubber rings of
treadbare tyres. 'The only element of everyday life that I
have never seen successfully integrated into a garden is the
car.' Williams, it was clear, had never visited J. G. Ballard in
Old Charlton Road, Shepperton.

The fifty-two acres of low-rise apartments, garden
areas, parking lots and lake, with which Carol was tasked in
Yonkers, felt like a tribute to her father, the architect Bronek
Katz, and his realisation of the Homes and Gardens Pavilion at the Festival of Britain in 1951. Williams found herself
translated into liminal territory: 'a city that has spread far
beyond its geographic borders.' Her instinct, making the
commute from her home in Sag Harbor, Long Island, was
that places that are not *seen*, that are not part of the public
debate, 'have become virtually uninhabitable'.

It is a large step, from the physical act of working one's
own ground, clearing, composting, planting, pruning,
picking and eating, to engaging with the politics of an
edgeland estate, a community of strangers. At home, Carol
tempered her own anaemic inclinations with tonic tea made

from the leaves of young nettles. She followed Rudolf Steiner in trying the experiment of grasping the nettles in her bare hands, and feeling, in the 'burn', homeopathic jolts of iron radiation, 'currents of potash and calcium'. Steiner compares the 'marvellous inner structure and way of working' of this plant with 'the heart in the human organism'.

In Yonkers, Carol certainly grasped the nettle of the real. She was responsible for improved systems of garbage disposal and collection. She walked and pondered and conceived new park areas and playgrounds. She investigated laundry rooms. 'I had to report that nothing *could* happen unless buildings, plantings, residents were *cared for.*' That was the simple and obvious conclusion: structures are never more than a manifestation of the attention given to them. The moral duty of the developer is to respond to the needs and requirements of those who take up residence, by choice or necessity, in their properties. Carol, as was inevitable, uncovered the fault lines in this system: bad practice, unchecked, shading into petty corruption and outright criminality. Garbage has a history of malevolence along the waterfront and through the boroughs. It no longer felt safe, Williams said, to continue her programme of attentive 'wandering through cellars and thickets', the expeditions that sustained her conception of a better way. And her firm resolve to create more shady corners, usable benches beside trees: 'homelike' details to ameliorate the atmosphere of menace.

The intrepid gardener captured maps and photographs displayed in the manager's office, helicopter sweeps over the original plot from the mid 1960s. She marked the boundaries with a green pen. Rents were low, the fabric was crumbling. Major highways, snaking through tract-land, enclose the estate. But there is breathing space left between the blocks – and variety. The Yonkers estate doesn't have the regimentation of a garden city, a nowhere strip, neither suburb nor country, waiting for the metropolis to stretch out and absorb it. There are more than a thousand apartments and some of the tenants have been there for fifty years. The battles, as Carol who grew up in London, and who made irregular visits across the pond, knew very well, were everywhere now. Skirmishes lost are still important: they keep our attention on malpractice and reflex mendacity.

WHEN REBECCA HIND received the medical verdict, it came out of nowhere. And it struck so perversely against the grain of her present happiness and the fulfilment of work, journeys, visions and intimate friendships. The path she could see opening up ahead. Unable or unwilling to tolerate the chemotherapy regime on offer, she determined to deal with the intruder in her own way, avoiding intrusive surgery and making a number of trips to a specialist German clinic run by Dr Herzog, where she received four treatments of hyperthermia/chemotherapy, or induced fever, under which the saving poisons are delivered. The full range of complementary practices, including reflexology and magnetic field therapy, were experienced. Rebecca went to Heathrow in a wheelchair and returned home, revived, to Dorchester; energised and hungry to continue. To swim. To travel. To draw. To keep company with her friends.

I couldn't help thinking again about what Anna Seghers wrote in *Transit*: 'I said that medicine didn't work. That, in fact, it didn't really exist. That no person had ever actually been cured by a physician, that people got well as a result of some coincidence or other.'

When I saw Rebecca at an Oxford book launch for her partner and lover, Brian Catling, she was smiling, immaculately presented and in good spirits, but visibly, now, melting away. Pressed to take a glass of wine, she accepted, but barely put her lips to the rim. The physical mantle was dissolving, almost hour by hour.

I continued to make afternoon visits to Hawksmoor's Spitalfields church. Ava sat at her desk on the right of the entrance, guardian of the papers, keeper of history. 'Do you like music?' With every passing day, we advanced a little beyond this riddle. I understood that the church required a gatekeeper. Ava had come from Calcutta, in the grip of belief or transmitted vision, with no intention of staying or attaching herself to this place, a penance she accepted with good grace. It was said, and she confirmed it to me, that in the past, in the limbo of the building's long ruin, when it was locked against intruders, she *lived* here. In some side chamber or cupboard or organ loft. That is what she had been instructed by her god to do. She took the entire building, the grandeur of the nave, its columns, the gold and the white, the heraldic devices, city pomp and chandeliers, galleries and stained glass, as destiny. The details of sepulchral monuments, the watercolour triptych before the altar, those things did not concern her.

The way the keepers chose to light the building, the high theatre of it, affected the balance and subtlety of Hind's *Scintilla*. The shadow of that brazen symbol, the polished cross of sacrifice, intruded on the central panel of the painting, making it appear that the diagonal thread of Hind's lightning stoke – 'transverse zig-zaggery' – was performing a 'passion play' strike on the altar of Christ Church.

There had been a difficulty, Catling told me, with the installation of the central arched panel. Hind was given the wrong measurements. Brian scrolled through his laptop to show me a sequence of joyous photographs of the paintings in progress on the floor of the deserted summer studio of the sculpture department of the Ruskin School of Drawing and Fine Art at Bullingdon Road in Oxford. Rebecca pours, evaluates, moves, laughs, mixes – reaches out for one of the thick brushes. And then, coming to Spitalfields, she had to trim her composition with a blade on a stick: a one-shot risk she accomplished with Zen mastery.

The three *Scintilla* panels are windows accepting the thin donations of light carried to the building by visitors – but they are open, at the same time, to the courtship of elemental forces, furnace and thunder cloud: uncontainable energies pouring through the watercolour catchment from behind, from outside. The 'Birth' panel, on the left as you approach, is a cauldron of generating fire with traceries of 'glittering specks' flying upward. The vitalist *actions* of the making are implicit in our bedazzled contemplation of the slowed expenditure of time in the finished paintings.

'Ever constant, yet in perpetual change,' Rebecca's son, Tom Kevin Slingsby, wrote of *Bright Sun Rising* in the Lady Chapel at Dorchester. He saw the 'numinous site-specific artwork … shining out from below the stained glass window'. The painting was 'an alternate light source'. He made a comparison with the experience of staring without blinking into an open fireplace. Tom described his mother's intention of contriving 'an integrated permanence … designed to cohere stylistically with the architecture … to reflect and magnify the ritual and special ambience'.

The Christ Church triptych is a cascade of waterlight *scintillating* against the assertive grandeur of Hawksmoor, that masculine insistence on 'terror and magnificence': a space stripped and painted for concerts, promotions and televised incantations. A ballroom of vanities in which I remember seeing the magus Alan Moore marking out a pentagram of spectral conjurings for the camera.

As with Carol Williams and her garden, Hind's magic was in the act of making, not the finished product – which was a record of process, the chart of a stage towards something unreachable. The act was a discipline and a strike at the dark: repeated washes, graduated tonal richness, colour glowing through colour. The stabbing and scratching away with the head of a drill. Catling remembers the steady hum of Rebecca's enraptured concentration as she flickered between the motif and the hungry porous paper.

I have looked at the sketch book for *Scintilla* and some of the preliminary watercolours. Hind knew the history of the Hawksmoor space, its power and its challenges. She attended a performance by her daughter Holly who was living and working in the neighbourhood. Holly's intention, she told me, was to challenge 'verticality'. She mixed glitter with ash, anticipating – before Rebecca's *Scintilla* commission – flakes of future fire drifting down like burning snow through the hollow body of the church.

There is a black sketchbook from 2007 entitled FIRE: SPITALS. NIGHT SPHERES FORGE. Hind's flames are teased and flicked from colour washes. Her sparks are released through accumulated layers by deft strokes from a Dremel tool. When the artist used this instrument to duplicate the shock-waves of hundreds of starlings suddenly appearing over Lindisfarne, Prince Charles, touring the Dorchester exhibition in which the painting was shown, bent stiffly forward to proclaim: 'How brave!' Techniques have been rehearsed and mastered. The *Scintilla* panel representing 'Death' is all sky. But the thin bed of ground where the lightning strikes is a placid English field.

'In her images the body is gone,' Catling wrote in the leaflet that accompanied the original 2010 exhibition. The one that Ava excavated from the locked cupboard. 'She has chosen the reincarnation of light to illuminate ... existence.' Nature's wilful energies are suspended in the physics of perception. Familiar landscapes and cloudscapes, witnessed and recorded in Hind's panels, only confirm an abiding absence. But an absence without shame or fear.

In a brown pocketbook titled 'Large Painting Log', Hind kept a meticulous, day-by-day, action-by-action, account of the evolution of the commission. Recipes from which the watercolours can be dissolved into their constituent parts. 'Fading to dark tertiary. Dried overnight ... 8 layers = one too much ... Flames re-established ... Lost something ... Need to do more pouring ... '

I DROVE TO OXFORD to spend a day with Catling. He has Rebecca's painting of the explosion of Lindisfarne starlings, experienced in Gertrude Jekyll's garden at the back of the castle, in his bedroom. His shaded window, reflected in the glass of the framed watercolour, makes a narrow door into the scene, the dark Northumbrian sky. With Hind, there are always landscapes behind landscapes, nothing is fixed or final. Clouds become firm ground, before they begin to melt and boil. Or before they part for an instant to reveal a luminescent moon-shell or the flaring, liquid rim of the sun.

We ran through hundreds of photographs of works made on holidays and sketching tours. I took one of the smiling portraits – Rebecca in hard-weather anorak, sitting on stone, turning and tilting to face the camera – to be on a mountain top, with a black fist of cloud floating above. But it was a Scottish shore. The clouds were in the black water. The mysterious object was seaweed or the head of a rock. The tall thin strip of the photograph mimics the shape of the central Christ Church panel.

The shelves of the Oxford house were freighted with many remembrances of Rebecca Hind, not least the flurry of small paintings that Catling was now producing. There had been conversations on technique and trips to look at buildings and artworks. At one point, Hind tried a few abortive technical lessons on her partner.

'As you know, I keep myself out of what I write,' Brian said. But that exposed self, or some projected version of it, was making an insistent appearance in poems drawing on the overwhelming experience of love and loss. He called his recent paintings, sampling and shifting memories from early Italian and Dutch sources, 'medieval conversations between the unshriven, the quick and the dead'. The paintings were also illuminations for unwritten books. Forests. Doors. Deaths. And resurrections.

The series that took my immediate attention could have come from our pilgrimage to the Hebrides. Catling found

the source photographs, captured on a recent expedition –
huts, shacks, abandoned nests of failed survivalists – in the
Mojave desert and the snows of Connecticut. After being
with Rebecca as she faded away, physically, while calling for
parties and gatherings of family and friends, Brian needed
to be somewhere different: he posted road footage from a
barren land, heading for Death Valley. 'Who is driving?'
we all said. And then the camera moved across for the
big reveal: Catling. Universal shock waves. *Noooooo!* To
witness the always chauffeured poet/performer at the wheel
was world changing. Like discovering that Flann O'Brien,
in the depths of his Dalkey inebriation, was right all along:
James Joyce *was* a barman in Skerries.

Catling's imploded shack paintings were portraits
of people we would never see. The toothpick fragility of
structures erected to give shelter against the elements and
furies had caved in like a face with water for bones. The
Connecticut cabin is almost inhabitable, a square hide, its
right angles tilted and crazy. The Mojave prospector's hut
is a shell left by bomb tests and picked apart by vultures.
Shadows run into the sand like spills of tar. With a magni-
fying glass I can make out some Manson-era signage on a
standing wall: WELCOME HOME.

WE HEADED OUT to inspect *transi* monuments. The alabas-
ter skin of Alice de la Pole in Ewelme was unusual in its
silken reality, the stalled breath of both living and dead
versions, when set against the broken double effigy of the
male knight at Fyfield, with his missing limbs. The house
of death, maquette for immortality, was shaken; structural
cracks threatened to bring the whole contrivance down.
Alice was a woman of power from a great political dynasty.
Catling explained that her wealth was used to create a spectacle, a presentation intended to strike visitors dumb, and
to ensure constant prayers for the release of the aristocrat's
soul from purgatory. The latest egg tempera paintings in his

Oxford house focused on the post-mortem visions of that forensically realised skull in the tomb, her star-speckled ceiling burning needle holes through the lid to reveal the frozen darkness of the heavens above. Alice de la Pole was her own architect and this low-rise sepulchre, in which her sculpted effigy was placed, was a case study for any discussion of buildings, art and health.

Over a pub lunch, and reminiscences about our canoe voyage, Oxford to Dorchester, Catling spoke about Rebecca's time in the city of my birth, Cardiff, where Kevin Slingsby had worked for a time. Rebecca formed a close and enduring friendship with the artist Sue Williams. Together, after Kevin's death, the two women drove to Penarth, to the site where the exiled Impressionist Alfred Sisley made a series of paintings of the mouth of the Severn. Rebecca addressed a letter, not to be read by anyone else, to her dead husband's disease. Echoing a series of images Slingsby had produced of object-projectiles, this private missive was strapped to a brick, before being flung into the sea.

'Did I tell you what happened when I tried to take Rebecca out in the canoe?' Brian said. He had, several times. But it was a great story and I wanted to hear it again. He thought the borrowed vessel must have shrunk or warped in some way, in the years between the two voyages. He tried to sit, midships, but he was bigger now: he wedged. The seating plank gave way beneath him. He couldn't move. His struggles wrecked the fragile craft. The canoe filled with water and slowly sunk. Rebecca, watching from the bank, was helpless with laughter.

WHEN I RETURNED, for one last visit to Christ Church, Ava was not at her desk. The spotlights were switched off. I was free to sit and watch the *Scintilla* triptych without the intrusive shadows and the tripled crucifix. The strange Easter Island mask had disappeared from the central 'Death' panel. But as I stared, with half-shut eyes at 'Resurrection',

Scintilla triptych by Rebecca Hind. Christ Church, Spitalfields.

on the right, I experienced a compelling optical illusion. The heavy, vaporous cloud base began to lighten and the corona of the sun, its golden aureole, rose by degrees, a quite distinct movement, from behind thinner, pink clouds.

I had been told that Ava was a lover of cricket and I looked forward to hearing her views on recent events in South Africa, the sandpaper and the tears of the Australian miscreants. Her absence, in this vaulted space, was loud. She had become an important part of this equation. 'I think she's disappeared back to Pakistan for a break,' said the man with the keys. 'She comes and goes like a rent collector.'

Repeated attendance on Hind's triptych was a journey of blind faith. Something in the landscape was broken, but there was no healing in it for me. And no door opened in the masonry, there was no vision of a radiant city. Brian Catling, who witnessed the genesis of the Spitalfields watercolours, understood the process much better than I did. 'Each mark she makes is a signature of being here … asking water to paint flame as the sparks fly upwards.' He wrote a poem to be read at Rebecca's Dorchester funeral, which was attended by a large gathering of friends and admirers. 'This is how we will remember light,' he concluded.

'I can't imagine how you found the strength to read it.'

'I didn't,' he said. 'I passed the duty on.'

THE BOOK WAS FINISHED. I printed out the last sheets and came back to business and faced my emails. There was a message from Steve Dilworth. Joan had died that day. Steve held her hand, he said, as they listened to Arvo Pärt from the *Silence into Light* CD. Joan enjoyed the singing with Kötting so much, it was a special moment. The Estonian composer told an interviewer that his inspiration, the portal into timelessness, came from hearing three notes repeated on the public address system of a supermarket: the building block for music in the Western world drowned out the telltale hammering of his living heart.

Catling spoke, on the phone, to Dilworth in Harris, as snow fell, and the Scottish motorways were blocked with stalled convoys, the airports shut. 'Joan,' Dilworth said, 'is present now in the room.' In fact, migrations done, she is the house.

Select Bibliography

Beckett, Samuel, *All that Fall* (Faber & Faber, 1957).

Benjamin, Walter, *The Storyteller* (Verso, 2016).

Browne, Sir Thomas, *The Major Works* (Penguin Books, 1997).

—, *Religio Medici and Urne-Buriall*, edited by Stephen Greenblatt and Ramie Targoff (New York Review Books Classics, 2012).

Catling, B., *The Vorrh* (Coronet, 2015).

—, *The Erstwhile* (Coronet, 2017).

Dorn, Edward, *Recollections of Gran Apachería* (Turtle Island, 1974).

Eliade, Mircea, *Shamanism: Archaic Techniques of Ecstasy* (Routledge & Kegan Paul, 1964)

Hanley, Lynsey, *Estates: An Intimate History* (Granta, 2007).

Hoare, Philip, *Spike Island: The Memory of a Military Hospital* (Fourth Estate, 2001).

—, *England's Lost Eden: Adventures in a Victorian Utopia* (Fourth Estate, 2005).

—, *Leviathan, or, The Whale* (Fourth Estate, 2008).

—, *RISINGTIDEFALLINGSTAR* (HarperCollins, 2017).

Hodgson, William Hope, *The House on the Borderland* (Chapman & Hall, 1908).

Hutchinson, Roger, *The Soap Man: Lewis, Harris and Lord Leverhulme* (Birlinn, 2003).

Jasanoff, Maya, *The Dawn Watch: Joseph Conrad in a Global World* (Penguin Random House, 2017).

Kötting, Andrew, Mark Lythgoe, et al., *Mapping Perception* (Proboscis, 2002).

Lawrence, D. H., *The Plumed Serpent* (Martin Secker, 1926).

London, Jack, *The People of the Abyss,* (1903; Tangerine Press reissue, 2014). With original photographic plates.

Long, Haniel, *The Marvellous Adventures of Cabeza de Vaca* (Souvenir Press, 1972).

Luskacova, Markéta, *Photographs of Spitalfields*, with introductory essay by David Widgery (Whitechapel Art Gallery, 1991).

Macfarlane, Robert, *The Old Ways* (Hamish Hamilton, 2012).

Meades, Jonathan, *Peter Knows What Dick Likes* (Paladin Books, 1989).

—, *Museum Without Walls* (Unbound, 2012).

—, *An Encyclopaedia of Myself* (Fourth Estate, 2014).

Miles, Barry, *Ginsberg: A Biography* (Penguin, 1990).

Molina, Antonio Muñoz, *Like a Fading Shadow.* (Farrar, Straus and Giroux, 2017).

Moorhouse, Paul, *Leon Kossoff* (Tate Gallery Publications, 1996).

Petit, Chris, *Pale Horse Riding* (Simon & Schuster, 2017).

Pollard, Richard, *Hastings, Looking back to the Future: A tribute to Sidney Little* (Published by author, 2011).

Sbriglio, Jacques, *Le Corbusier: L'Unité d'habitation de Marseille* (Birkhäuser, 2004).

Sebald, W. G., *The Rings of Saturn* (Eichborn, 1998).

—, *Austerlitz* (C. Hanser, 2001).

Seghers, Anna, *Transit* (1944; New York Review Books Classics, 2013).

Sinclair, Iain, *Lud Heat: A Book of the Dead Hamlets* (Albion Village Press, 1975).

—, *White Chappell, Scarlet Tracings* (Goldmark, 1987).

— (ed.), *London: City of Disappearances* (Hamish Hamilton, 2006).

Stevenson, Robert Louis, *The Suicide Club* and *The Rajah's Diamond* (London Magazine, 1894).

Widgery, David, *Some Lives! A GP's East End* (Trafalgar Square Publishing, 1991).

—, *Against Miserabilism: Writings 1968–1992* (Vagabond Voices, 2017).

Willes, Margaret, *The Curious World of Samuel Pepys and John Evelyn* (Yale University Press, 2017).

Willetts, Paul, *Fear and Loathing in Fitzrovia: The Bizarre Life of Julian Maclaren-Ross* (revised edition) (Dewi Lewis Publishing, 2005).

Williams, Carol, *Bringing a Garden to Life* (Bantam Books, New York, 1998).

Acknowledgements

LIVING WITH BUILDINGS was a commissioned project. My thanks to Kirty Topiwala, publisher at Wellcome Collection, for allowing me to find my own tracks across unfamiliar territory, while keeping a map of established directions and compass bearings firmly in hand. To Penny Daniel and Valentina Zanca at Profile Books. And to those tactful mediators, my agents Laura Longrigg and Diana Tyler.

I owe much of the original impetus in this book to the paintings of Rebecca Hind and the sculpture of Steve Dilworth. And to Brian Catling, who was unstinting in his support, a constantly replenished store of images and information. Andrew Kötting was both a dynamic companion and goad for many miles; his memories of the Bence House days fired any understanding I have of the Pepys Estate. Eden Kötting was, as ever, Andrew's muse and accomplice. Emma Matthews, champion of resistance at Bowater House, found time, at this most challenging moment, to answer questions and provide documentation of the struggles at Golden Lane. Philip Hoare, fellow traveller in Mexico, was the ideal guide to Southampton Water and the ghosts of the Royal Military Hospital at Netley. For generous hospitality, I would like to thank Jonathan Meades and Colette Forder in Marseille and Steve and Joan Dilworth on the Isle of Harris.

Carol Williams points out that the defensive notion of burying Hawksmoor's Christ Church originated with her husband, Hugh Williams. And this is true. I don't believe Carol would have initiated such a dramatic cancellation of a landmark building. But, within the specific context of this unravelling history, I decided to stick with my 'alternative fact' version, and not to complicate the already stretched narrative thread by introducing yet another unexplained character. My apologies to Hugh. The shock of your vision, in all its initial confidence, stays with me.

Many thanks to Leon Kossoff for permission to reproduce one of the drawings of Christ Church, Spitalfields. This series and the paintings derived from them helped to anchor the tentative opening movements of the book. I am grateful to Andrea Rose for her assistance in accessing this drawing.

For permission to quote from David Widgery, I would like to thank Juliet Ash. For other quotations I would like to express my obligation to Brian Catling, Philip Hoare, Andrew Kötting, Jonathan Meades, Barry Miles, Antonio Muñoz Molina, Chris Petit and Carol Williams.

Anthony O'Donnell (Anonymous Bosch) provided a file of inimitable photographs from the expedition to the Hebrides. Anna Sinclair, once again, was the companion, sharer, conscience, and occasional tolerator of eccentricities, in this project.

For other reasons of help, hospitality, ideas and information, I would like to thank Michael Curran, Richard and Susa Ellis, Gareth Evans, Robert Hadman, Bill Parry-Davies, Macgillivray, Robert Macfarlane, Juan Manuel and Claudia Franco Franco, Manuel Ramirez Martinez, Louis Petit, Holly Slingsby, Tom Slingsby, Sue Williams, Alan Moore and Ken Worpole.

List of Illustrations

Frontispiece: Leon Kossoff, Christ Church, Spitalfields, 1991, charcoal on paper © Leon Kossoff. Reproduced with permission.

p. 11   'In the Shadow of Christ's Church, I Saw', JLP 466 Alb. 28 #03636. Jack London papers, The Huntington Library, San Marino, California.

p. 11   'A Chill, Raw Wind Was Blowing ...', JLP 466 Alb. 28 #03584 ibid.

p. 13   'View in Spitalfields', JLP 466 Alb. 28 #03578 op cit.

p. 31   Pepys Estate, Deptford, London: children playing on a raised walkway, Tony Ray-Jones / RIBA Collections.

p. 31   Pepys Estate, Deptford, London: schoolboy in his living room, Tony Ray-Jones / RIBA Collections.

p. 33   William Price of Llantrisant (1800–1893) MRCS, LSA, medical practitioner, in druidic costume, with goats. Oil painting by A. C. Hemming. Wellcome Collection.

p. 35   Plaque on Walworth Clinic wall (1937). Photograph by Ken Worpole.

p. 46   Bence House, Pepys Estate. Author photograph.

p. 48   The re-enactment of Rembrandt's *The Anatomy Lesson* from Mapping Perception, Andrew Kötting. Reproduced with permission.

p. 54   Stone carved skull from victually yard, Pepys Estate. Author photograph.

p. 55   Pepys Estate, first published in *Pepys Estate a GLC housing project*. Lewisham Local History and Archive Centre, London Borough of Lewisham. With Permission.

p. 58   Plan of Sayes Court, illustration from the 'Evelyn Papers', *c*.1653–4 (pen & ink on paper), Evelyn, John (1620–1706) / British Library, London, UK / © British Library Board. All Rights Reserved / Bridgeman Images.

p. 63   View of Golden Lane Estate (SC/PHL/02/0736/71/3568), Goswell Road, London Metropolitan Archives, City of London.

p. 68   Golden Lane Estate, protest banners. Photo by Charles Humphreys.

p. 75   Portrait of Emma and Louis Petit by Katherine Fawssett. Copyright © Katherine Fawssett.

p. 78   Demolition of Golden Lane Estate. Photo by Charles Humphreys.

p. 82   Barbican water. Author photograph.

p. 86   Le Corbusier sketch of Unite d'habitation, © FLC/ADAGP, Paris and DACS, London 2018.

p. 98   Statue, Notre-Dame de la Garde basilica, Marseille. Author photograph.

p. 99   Six views of Le Block Corbusier, Marseille. Author photographs.

p. 123 Netley Hospital, contemporary postcard, Wellcome Collection.

p. 127 Philip Hoare's hand. Photograph by Philip Hoare.

p. 129 Steve Dilworth's *Whalebone Box*. Photograph by Anonymous Bosch. Reproduced with permission.

p. 133 The Hebrides. Photos by Anonymous Bosch. Reproduced with permission.

p. 139   Rebecca Hind, *Bright Rising*, 2013. Watercolour on paper, reredos at Dorchester Abbey. Reproduced with kind permission.

p. 141   *Hanging Figure* by Steve Dilworth. Photograph by Steve Dilworth. Reproduced with permission.

p. 145   Whalebox burial. Author photograph.

p. 151   Rebecca Hind at work. Reproduced with kind permission.

p. 165   Rebecca Hind, *Scintilla: the glittering speck*, 2010. Watercolour on paper, reredos at Christ Church Spitalfields, London.

While every effort has been made to contact copyright-holders of illustrations, the author and publishers would be grateful for information about any illustrations where they have been unable to trace them, and would be glad to make amendments in further editions.

Living with Buildings: an exhibition about health and architecture

THIS BOOK WAS FIRST PUBLISHED on the occasion of *Living with Buildings* an exhibition at Wellcome Collection. The exhibition explores the interaction of health and architecture from the slums of nineteenth-century London to contemporary healing spaces for cancer patients. Approaches of architects, planners and designers can have a powerful influence over our feelings of individual wellbeing, as well as physical health and have much to tell us about the dominant wider priorities in society and politics.

In the introduction to the publication of *Oliver Twist*, some thirty years after it first appeared as a serial, Charles Dickens wrote: 'Nothing can be done for the elevation of the poor in England, until their dwelling places are made decent and wholesome.' This statement illustrates the close connection between housing, politics, health – and the role artists, writers and filmmakers can have in drawing out the voices of those living in unsafe housing. A line can be drawn between Dickens' words to the terrible fire at Grenfell Tower in June 2017. The tower block, a utopian dream born out of post war planning and visions of modernity, has become a symbol of the failure of architecture to address social need. On one hand the tragic events at Grenfell reinforce the inhospitality of the twentieth century tower block, but a community has been revealed that challenges the dominant narrative that the shape of the building you live in somehow defines your value in society.

Architecture also has a role to play in the delivery of health care. The Modernist designs for the health centres at Peckham and Finsbury were shaped by their individual purpose to promote health and combat disease. Contemporary 'super' hospitals provide treatment for the masses, but can lack the intimacy and humanity of smaller spaces. Cancer charity Maggie's has pioneered a model in which architecture and design can offer a different kind of care in a different kind of space, one in which individuality, humanity and empathy are placed centre stage.

Living with Buildings tells the stories of these structures – and the people who use them – and many more besides. The exhibition traces how urban planning and development has been employed as a tool to improve people's lives, as well as showing how architecture can respond to global issues in health today.

Emily Sargent

Index

Note: Where friends are referred to by their given names alone, they are either accessible by those names or cross-referenced from them. Thus Carol Williams is at both C and W. Italic page numbers indicate illustrations.

A

Ackroyd, Peter, *Hawksmoor* 15
Alice de la Pole 163–4
Alice in Wonderland, dir. Jonathan Miller 122, 125
Alice in Wonderland syndrome 78
Alÿs, Francis 115
Amis, Martin, *London Fields* 6
amphetamine (benzedrine) 22–4
Andrew (Kötting) *see* Kötting
Anna (Sinclair) 90, 95, 101
Anthony (O'Donnell) 130, 146, 148
Aragon, Louis, *Paris Peasant* 55

Aragon Tower 55–7
Arnold Circus 10, 14–15, 155
Ash, Juliet 17
Ava (Christ Church custodian) 152–3, 158–9, 161, 166

B

Ballachulish 140–1
Ballard, J(ames) G(raham) 8, 93–5, 156
Super-Cannes 93–4
Ballard, Jean 94
Barbers' Physic Garden 81–3
Barbican development 63–4, 71–2, 78, 79, 81–2, 82
barnacle geese 82
Bateson, Gregory 84
Beckett, Samuel, *All That Fall* (radio play) 24

Bedlam / Bethlem Hospital
81, 124

beggars *see* vagrants

Bence House, Deptford
44–5 46, 48–50, 52

Benjamin, Walter 28, 88–90

benzedrine (amphetamine)
22–4

Berkeley Homes 56–7

Bernard Morgan House
64–5, 67–8

Betjeman, John 29, 51–2, 57

Blake, William 15, 16, 45, 62

bodies, disposal 50

body-snatchers 18

Böll, Heinrich 91

Bond, Martin 56

Boukobza, Fernand 101

Bowater House 64–8, *68*, 71,
74, 77–8, 101

Brian (Catling) *see* Catling

Bright Rising, by Rebecca
Hind 139, *139*, *160*

British Medical Association
32, 37

Brookes, Les 57

Browne, Sir Thomas
33, 47, 53, 59–60, 70

brutalism 51, 63–4, 67, 82, *86*

Burghley, Lord (William Cecil)
83

burial, proposed, of buildings
25, 155

Burroughs, William 8

Burton, James 36–8

Burton St Leonards 38, 106

C

Campbell, Colin Ray 141

Camus, Albert 100

Carol (Williams) 20–3, 25,
155–8

Carroll, Lewis (Charles
Lutwidge Dodgson) 78

Casa Malaparte, Capri 105

Cathedral of the Assumption
of Our Lady, Guadalajara
117

Catherine of Aragon, Queen
56

Catling, Brian 147, 149,
151–2, 158–64, 166
appreciation of Rebecca
Hind's work 149–50,
161–2, 166
The Erstwhile 124, 127
Scintilla exhibition booklet
152, 161
Slingsby memorial 138–9

Cecil, William (Lord
Burghley) 83

Céline, Louis-Ferdinand 8

Cézanne, Paul 90

Chamberlin, Powell & Bon
62–4, 67, 82

Charles, Prince 161

Chepstow Place, Notting Hill
21–4

children
as register of an
environment 72
seaside memories 84–5

Christ Church, Spitalfields
3, 10, 12, 14–17, 20,
149–51
as 'Christ's Church' (Jack
London) 10–12
custodian (Ava) 152–3,
158–8, 161, 166
Scintilla triptych 3, 150–3,
159–61, 164–6, *165*
Cité Radieuse 85, 94, 97,
100–3, 109
see also Unité d'habitation
Cole, B(enjamin), engraving
15–16
Colette (Forder) 86, 94, 101,
104
communities, supportive
76–7
complementary medicine 158
Conrad, Joseph 21, 91–2, 135
Corbu *see* le Corbusier
council housing / estates
21, 44, 49–50, 52, 56–7, 66,
77
Coutard, Raoul 96
Coverley, Merlin,
Psychogeography 55
Cronin, Anthony, *Dead as
Doornails* 22
cultural memory 71, 142

D

Dalgleish, Kenneth 106
Dautry, Raoul 85, 89

The Denizen Estate
64–5, 72, 77
Dickens, Charles, *Oliver
Twist* 174
diets, demands of 74
Digby, Sir Kenelm 30, 33
Dilworth, Steve
Hanging Figure (sculpture)
135–6, *141*, 141–3
Off the Rock (exhibition)
137
whalebone box by *129*,
130, 136–48, *145*, 155
Dilworth, Steve and Joan
130, 132–8, 143, 146–8,
166–7
Döblin, Alfred, *Berlin
Alexanderplatz* 8, 89
Dorchester-on-Thames 138–
40, 158, 160–1, 164, 166
Bright Rising, by Rebecca
Hind 139, *139, 160*
Dorn, Ed, *Recollections of
Gran Apacheriá* 152
Drake, Sir Francis 56
Dupuytren's contracture 121

E

Eden (Kötting) 44–9, 51–2,
54, 59
Eliade, Mircea 25
Elliott, J Inness 65
Emma (Matthews) 67, 71–7,
75, 104, 121

An Englishman's Home
(documentary) 51–2
'Entelechia' 53
epilepsy / falling sickness /
seizures 65, 69, 73–4,
76–7, 81, 83
Equiano, Olaudah 56
Eric (uncle to Meades) 88
Espérandieu, Henri 97
estates, concept 38–9, 44,
49–51, 54, 59, 61, 66–7
see also Golden Lane;
Pepys
eugenicist viewpoints 14, 16
Evelyn, John 30, 36, 43–4,
58, 60–1
Fumifugium 27
see also Sayes Court
ex-voto offerings / paintings
32, 44, 97–8, 100, 119–20
exclusive districts 35–6

F

façadism 13
Fawssett, Katherine 75
Festival of Britain, 1951 156
films
The Beast in View (project)
22
Content, by Chris Petit 73
Gallivant, by Andrew
Kötting, 47, 52, 85, 142
Isle of Rust, by Jonathan
Meades 87, 130, 132

by Jean-Luc Godard 95–6,
105
Mapping Perception
project 47, 48
Forder, Colette 86, 94, 101,
104
Fortune Street Park 69, 78
Foster, Norman 96
Franco, Juan Manuel Franco
and Claudia 118

G

garden cities 67, 80, 157
gardens and gardening
18–19, 58–61, 156–7
Barbers' Physic Garden
81–3
Geocrab 143, 147
Gerard, John, *Herball, or
Generall Historie of
Plantes* 83
Gibbons, Grinling 56
Ginsberg, Allen 8
Glen Coe 140
Godard, Jean-Luc
A Bout de Souffle 95–6
Le Mépris 105
Golden Lane Estate 62–8,
63, 71–5, 79, 101
origins 67
Gray, Eileen 108–9
Green, A(nna) K(atherine) 89
Greenblatt, Stephen 70
Gregory, Philippa 115
Grenfell Tower 51, 94, 174

Guadalajara, Mexico
114–15, 117–18, 120

H

Hanley, Lynsey, *Estates, An Intimate History* 49–50, 52
Harris, Isle of 128–30, 134, 140–6, 148, 166
Harwood, Lee 6–7
Hawksmoor, by Peter Ackroyd 15
Hawksmoor, Nicholas
London churches other than Christ Church 17, 20, 25
St Anne's, Limehouse 5, 17–18, 20
see also Christ Church, Spitalfields
health
and architecture 125, 175
and guilt 71
and overwork 105
Hebrides
Skye 142
Western Isles 128–30, *133,* 134, 140–6, 148, 166
Highland clearances 131, 134, 141
Hind, Rebecca 139–40, *151,* 153, 155, 158
association with Brian Catling 149–50, 161–2, 166

Bright Rising 139, *139, 160*
Scintilla triptych 3, 150–3, 159–61, 164–6, *165*
Hoare, Philip 79, 85, 113–17, 119–24, 126–7
England's Lost Eden: Adventures in a Victorian Utopia 122
Spike Island, The Memory of a Military Hospital 114, 124
Hodgson, William Hope, *The House on the Borderland* 19
the homeless *see* vagrants
Honey, Andrew 61
hospitals
better avoided 6–7, 19, 71
visiting 33
see also Bedlam; Royal Military Hospital
housing as infirmity 5–6

I

Ivain, Gilles 46

J

James of the Glen 141–2
Jasanoff, Maya, *The Dawn Watch...* 91–2
Jeanneret, Charles-Édouard *see* Le Corbusier
Joubert syndrome 49

Juniper, Barrie 61

K

Katz, Bronek 21–2, 156
Kossoff, Leon 14–16
Kötting, Andrew
  Gallivant (film) 47, 52, 85,
    142
  Hebridean trip 130–2,
    142–4, 146–8
  Mapping Perception
    project 47, 48
  memories of Bence House /
    Pepys Estate 44–5, 48,
    48–50, 52–4, 59
Kötting, Eden 44–9, 51–2,
  54, 59

L

Ladbroke, Sir Robert 151
Laing, R(onald) D(avid) 126
Lawrence, D(avid) H(erbert),
  The Plumed Serpent 118
Le Brasilia 101
Le Corbusier (Charles-
  Édouard Jeanneret) 85–6,
    100–2, 108
  Cité Radieuse 85, 94,
    100–2, 109
  disciples 51, 62, 67–8
  modular proportions
    102
  see also Unité d'habitation
Leila (McMillan) 44–5, 49

Lenin (Vladimir Ilyich
  Ulyanov) 39
Leverhulme, Lord (William
  Hesketh Lever) 131–2, 135
Lewis, Isle of 128, *133*, 134,
  145, 148
libraries, compared with
  hospitals 7
Limehouse 8, 18–20
  St Anne's Church 5, 17–
    18, 20
Lindisfarne starlings 161–2
Little, Sidney 106–7
Living with Buildings
  exhibition 179–180
London, Jack 9–13
  The People of the Abyss
    9, *11*, 14
  photographs by *11, 13*
Long, Haniel 113
Louis (Petit) 71–5, 75, 77–8,
  104
Luskačová, Markéta,
  Photographs of Spitalfields
    9, 16–17
Lythgoe, Mark 47–8

M

Macfarlane, Robert 136–7,
  144
  The Old Ways 137
Maclaren-Ross, Julian 22–4
Maher, John 146
Manuel (Ramirez Martinez)
  118–20

Marías, Javier 122, 128
Marine Court, St Leonards
    38, 106–8
Marseille
    Anna Seghers and 80,
        90–1
    Cité Radieuse 85, 94, 97,
        100–3, 109
    home of Jonathan Meades
        85–90, 94–5, 97, 100,
        104
    Jean-Luc Godard and 96
    Joseph Conrad in 91–2
    Notre-Dame de la Garde
        92, 96–7, 98, 101
    see also Unité d'habitation
Martinez, Manuel Ramirez
    118–20
Matthews, Emma 67, 71–7,
    75, 104
    The Hunt for Moby-Dick
        121
McMillan, Leila 44–5, 49
McWhinnie, Donald and
    Pauline 24
Meades, Jonathan
    Ape Forgets Medication
        (exhibition) 103
    Golden Lane campaign
        67–8
    on the Hebrides 130, 132,
        134
    Isle of Rust (film) 87, 130,
        132
    in Marseille 85–7, 94–5,
        100–6, 108

Museum Without Walls
    105, 132
The Plagiarist in the
    Kitchen 103
memory as geographic 20
Mexico 44, 56, 90, 108, 116
    Guadalajara 114–15,
        117–18, 120
    Mexico City 115
    Teuchitlán and Los
        Guachimontes 118, 121
    Tlaquepaque 119–20
migraines 72–3, 77–8, 82
Miller, Jonathan, Alice in
    Wonderland 122, 125
Mirzoeff, Edward 51
Mojave Desert 163
Molina, Antonio Muñoz
    69–71, 79, 84
    Like a Fading Shadow 69
Moorhouse, Paul 15
Morrison, Arthur, Child of
    the Jago 10
Mountbatten, Louis Francis
    Albert Victor Nicholas
    (Earl Mountbatten of
    Burma) 53–5
MRU (Ministry of
    Reconstruction and Urban
    Planning) 89–90
muggings 6
mulberry trees 61

N

Nash, Fiorella 52

Nash, Paul   38, 140
Netley, Royal Military
    Hospital   85, 88, 113–14,
    117, 121–6, 123, 134
New York, Yonkers   155–7
Notre-Dame de la Garde,
    Marseille.   92, 96–7, 98,
    101

O

O'Donnell, Anthony
    (Anonymous Bosch)   130,
    146, 148
Orozco, José Clemente   117
Oxford   61, 138, 140, 149,
    158–9, 161–4

P

Peck, Sir Edward   151
Pepys, Samuel   30, 36, 43–4,
    59, 61
Pepys Estate, Deptford
    29–30, 31, 43–4, 48–56,
    54–5, 59
    Bence House   44–5 46,
        48–50, 52
    dockyard predecessor   43,
        54, 59
    original prospectus   53
Pepys Park   59
Peter The Great (Tsar)   56
Petit, Chris   66–7, 89, 104
    Content (film)   73

and Emma Matthews   43,
    66–7, 73, 104
Pale Horse Riding   43
Petit, Louis   71–8, 75, 104
Philip (Hoare)   79, 85, 113–
    17, 119–24, 126–7
photography and forgetting
    79–80
Pied Piper of Hamelin   82
pilgrimages / penitence
    4, 87, 96–7, 117, 128
plagiarism   83, 86, 103
plaques, heritage / memorial /
    blue   5, 35–6, 38–9, 81
police
    dormitory redevelopment
        64–5
    in Marseille and London
        93, 96, 152
    training facility   126
pollution
    dust   23, 67, 76, 89
    'homoepathic doses'
        28, 61, 156
    plastic   72, 128
    traffic   5, 72, 81
Pope-Hennessy, James   24–5
Powell, Geoffry   64
Price, William, of Llantrisant
    33, 34
public toilets   142–3, 154
Pullen, Roger K   106

Q

quackery 30, 73, 80

R

Radiant City *see* Cité
    Radieuse
rail travel 88–90, 114
Ray, James Earl 70
Ray-Jones, Tony 29–30, *31*
Rebecca (Hind) *see* Hind
Rembrandt, *The Anatomy*
    Lesson of Dr Nicolaes
    Tulp 47
Révoli, Henri 97
Richardson, Dorothy,
    Pilgrimage 36
Right to Buy scheme
    48, 57, 63
Rilke, Rainer Maria 27
'Ripper' murders 15, 154
rough sleepers *see* vagrants
Royal (Victoria) Military
    Hospital, Netley 85, 88,
    113–14, 117, 121–6, *123*,
    134
Royal Naval Dockyard 43,
    54, 59
the Royal Society 30
ruins, allure of 87, 124,
    128–35, *133*, 146, 148, 163

S

Sallis, James 79
Santa Inocencia 117
Sayes Court 30, 43, 56, *58*,
    59–61
Scintilla triptych, by Rebecca
    Hind 3, 150–3, 159–61,
    164–6, *165*
sea, urges to return 84–5, 113
Sebald, W(infried) G(eorg)
    9, 33, 47
    Austerlitz 7
Seghers, Anna 90–1, 108
    Transit 80, 90, 158
Sinclair, Anna 90, 95, 101
Sinclair, Iain
    London, City of
        Disappearances (ed) 21
    Lud Heat, A Book of the
        Dead Hamlets 19
    White Chappell, Scarlet
        Tracings 25
Sinclair House, Bloomsbury
    37–8
Skinners Estate 37–9
Slingsby, Kevin 138, 140, 164
Slingsby, Tom Kevin 160
Snyder, Gary 76
Southampton Water
    85, 113–15, 121–2, 126
St Anne's, Limehouse
    5, 17–18, 20
St Clement's Church, Rodel
    144

Stein, Gertrude, *Tender Button* 104
Steiner, Rudolph 20, 157
Steve (Dilworth) *see* Dilworth
Stevenson, Robert Louis
  Kidnapped 142
  Pope-Hennessy biography 25
  The Suicide Club 22–3
Stewart, James (James of the Glen) 141–2
Stornoway, Isle of Lewis 128
Strictly Come Dancing 149, 154
surveillance 29, 65, 88
swimming 64, 73, 84–7, 95, 106–9, 113–16, 121–2

T

Tarbert, Isle of Harris 128, 137, 143
Targoff, Ramie 70
Taylor Wimpey 64, 66, 68–9, 71
tennis / tennis courts 62, 66–7, 72–3, 100–2, 104

U

l'Unité d'habitation, Marseille
  concept and funding 85, 89–90, 100
  images *86, 99*
  Jonathan Meades and 68, 87, 94, 100–5, 108
related buildings 67, 101
  see also Cité Radieuse

V

vagrants (homeless, beggars, mendicants) 8, 10, 12, 20, 79, 92–3, 107, 117, 154
valerian, and rats 82

W

walking, as a defence 4, 7, 19, 25, 79, 143
the Walworth Clinic *109*
Wellcome Collection 32–3, 174
Welsh, Irvine 115
the whalebone box *129, 130,* 136–48, *145,* 155
whales 60, 114, 120
Widgery, David 3–6, 8–9, 16–18
  The Doctor is Sick (essay) 4–5
  Against Miserabilism 17
Willetts, Paul 22–3
Williams, Carol 20–3, 25, 155–8
  Bringing a Garden to Life 156
Williams, Sue 164
Williams, William Carlos 8